What to Say

FRATERNAL PROSE, POETRY *and* QUOTES

REVISED EDITION

with CEREMONIES

MACOY PUBLISHING
AND MASONIC SUPPLY CO., INC
RICHMOND, VIRGINIA

PRINTED IN THE UNITED STATES OF AMERICA

FOREWORD

THE requests for "another *Gems of Thought*" have been so numerous that we feel a longer delay in bringing out this new collection of poems and speeches for fraternal occasions would be a failure in our service to you.

This compilation has been carefully made to order to meet the needs you have expressed in your requests for "something different" for a regular occasion, or "something to fit" an unusual event in your activities. Considerable time and effort have gone into seeking and selecting material of genuine worth and usableness. May it be a real treasure trove and inspiration to fraternal officers who take pride in smooth and gracious presiding at meeting and social events.

The selections included have been so edited and arranged that the busy officer will find them ready for use without change; and those speakers who wish a more individualized expression of sentiment will discover both inspiration and a model on which to build their own presentations.

The greatest possible care has been taken to find the sources and to give credit to the authors of quoted material. We regret if we have inadvertently failed to give credit in cases where the source is known.

If you who have by your requests inspired the compilation of this volume find in it the fulfillment of your expressed needs then *What To Say* requires no further justification for its launching at this time.

THE PUBLISHERS.

CONTENTS

I

WELCOMES

ONE who has heard the word "welcome" can never again be counted a stranger. Welcome is the keynote of hospitality. It connotes open doors, friendly greetings, sincere handclasps. All of these we extend to you and bid you welcome.

———

A little said, and truly said,
Can deeper joy impart
Than hosts of words that reach the lips
But come not from the heart.

———

While "guest" is a most gracious word
We would not call you thus.
While you are here we'd have you know
That you are one of us.
We want you to feel without a doubt
That our welcome is sincere—our latchstring is out.
We are giving you smiles that come from within
And hope we may greet you again and again.

———

A Chinese philosopher has said "A stranger may give bread but a welcome comes only from the lips of friendship."

———

No sweeter word falls upon the listening ear than the word welcome. It possesses magical power; it quickens the mind to keenest interest and lulls the heart with its soothing sound.

There is no word I know
Which makes the heart glad, where'er you go,
Like this word "welcome," rightly said.

Next to "home" and "mother," "welcome" is the sweetest word in our language.

There is magic in the word "welcome" that makes us forget the word "stranger" and causes us to remember that we are sisters banded together for the good of humanity. We want you to partake of our hospitality and hope that your visit here may ever remain with you a happy memory.

It is a great honor and privilege to greet you and I only wish it were in my power to more fittingly express what is in my heart. The officers and members of ———— Chapter join with me whole-heartedly in extending to you a warm and cordial welcome.

No greater privilege can come to a Worthy Matron than that of welcoming the Past Matrons and Past Patrons of the Chapter which they have served so well and so faithfully. Tonight we pay tribute to the devoted service you have rendered. You have made our Chapter what it is today.

We want you to know, as the years go by,
That the ties of the past hold true,
And deep in our hearts there's a place set aside
That we'll always keep just for you.

Today welcomes Yesterday and asks leave to walk by its side toward the glory of Tomorrow.

———

Welcome isn't a big word—it has only seven letters—but it covers a world of love and thankfulness. Once a year it is our privilege to have with us our Past Matrons and Past Patrons, those valiant soldiers who have battled so earnestly for the good and welfare of our Chapter. You have retired to the ranks of those whose year of leadership is over but there has never been a time when you were not ready and willing to give counsel and assistance when called upon. So it is with heartfelt gratitude that we welcome you here tonight.

Our thoughts of some folks never change,
And all good friends are always dear;
But knowing you, it isn't strange
That we should love you more each year.

———

In behalf of ———— Chapter I extend to you a sincere and heartfelt welcome. We have looked forward to this night of your coming with great anticipation. May our deeds as well as our words show the pleasure we feel in having you with us. I know everyone present will join in making this meeting one to be remembered. Let me assure you that we meet you in Truth, greet you in Faith and welcome you in Love. Emerson once wrote in his diary: "I like people who can do things." You have our respect and our love for your untiring efforts and excellent service in behalf of our beloved Order. Yours is the arduous task of ironing out the difficulties and misunderstandings in our Chapters and encouraging and inspiring them to higher goals. Your reward is the satisfaction that comes with the knowledge of a task well done. Your presence here is an inspiration to us and to all who come in contact with you. I bid you a most cordial welcome.

―――

It brings a glow of happiness to my heart to extend fraternal greetings to you. This room is full of welcome. May every hour you are with us prove an inspiration to us all and may we carry away from this meeting only pleasant memories and a deeper love for our beautiful Order.

―――

We are happy to welcome our Grand Representative tonight. Grand Representatives have a unique place in the Eastern Star. Their work is international and as far reaching as Stardom itself. They are the links which bind the Stars of every state and nation together. It is their duty to keep us informed of the many interesting events that take place in the state or country they represent. Their office is an important one and we are proud to honor our Sister who is our special guest tonight. We want you to have a big year. May you gain new friends by thousands and lose not one of the old; may you receive many blessings and have no heartaches. We want your year to be a model for future administrations, and may we stand by this *― and this*―and this*―and this*―and this*―. [The Star points give their signs, each being held until all have finished.]

―――

You need no words of mine to assure you that you are welcome to this Chapter. However, every home must have a hostess, and it is my happy privilege to open wide the door to you and, with a heart full of love, bid you welcome. The service you have given has been without thought of self but for the advancement of this beautiful Order, and because of the unselfishness of this service each one of us has experienced much of real joy.

> May the Star which we follow throughout every year
> Shine down on your life, bringing comfort and cheer;
> May the links we have added to Friendship's bright chain
> Grow brighter each year, and forever remain;
> May the strength you have given, the hours you have spent,
> Reflect on your life, bringing peace and content;
> May the heavenly Father, Whose love we all know,
> Comfort and guard you wherever you go.

————

Worthy Grand Matron, it is with pride and the greatest of pleasure that I welcome you to ———— Chapter tonight. Your title denotes the years of loyal service you have given to this great Order and we are assured you merit the high honor which has been bestowed upon you. We feel highly honored to have you visit us. Your coming attests the interest you take in our Chapter and I assure you this interest is greatly appreciated. We are very happy to have you with us. We hope your visit will be a most pleasant one and that you will carry away with you sweet memories of our Chapter that will never be forgotten.

————

To many we merely nod in passing, others we clasp by the hand, but our sincere and true friends are welcomed through our Chapter door, and because that friend is you, our hearts are filled with happiness as we bid you welcome.

As we go through life we find no word that gives us greater joy than the word "welcome," and so we want to say that word to you tonight. But mere words can never express to you the joy we feel at having you with us. It is through the friendly smile, the warm handclasp, and the spirit of love in our members that a real welcome can be expressed. Such is the greeting we extend to you this evening.

———

In behalf of ——— Chapter I bid you a sincere welcome. We appreciate your kindness in coming to us and know it is another expression of your love for, and devotion to, our beautiful Order.

———

II

RESPONSES TO WELCOME

YOUR gracious words of welcome ring with earnestness and sincerity. I assure you I deeply appreciate the fraternal spirit shown in your most cordial welcome—and thank you.

———

When spoken in sincerity and love the word "welcome" is one of surpassing beauty. Your fraternal love, your strong, warm handclasps and your gracious greeting have filled our hearts with gratitude, for we know yours is a true welcome.

———

God wove a web of loveliness of clouds and stars and birds, but made not anything as beautiful as words—the most beautiful of which is the word "welcome." It holds the warmth of fellowship and love and brings to our hearts a glow of happiness, for when we are greeted with the word welcome we know we are with friends.

———

I thank you for your welcome. Welcome—the sweetest word in the English language—and when uttered with the utmost sincerity, as it has been here tonight, it carries its message from heart to heart.

———

It would be futile for me to attempt to adequately express in words my appreciation of the gracious welcome just ac-

7

corded me. The warmth and sincerity of your greeting fills me with joy and will ever remain with me as a fragrant flower from our garden of fraternity.

———

I thank you for every courtesy you have extended to me. Words cannot tell the joy your flowers give to me. They will fade but their fragrance will live in my memory forever.

———

My heartstrings are pulling too tight for words. I just want to say that I want you for my friends—I need every one of you —so that together we may go ahead and make the coming year one of helpfulness and friendliness.

———

Your welcoming voice—the touch of your hand—
Is the greeting the heart can best understand.

———

I thank you for your warm welcome. I have looked forward to this evening for a long time. It is the help and inspiration received from Chapters such as this that give me the courage to continue in the path of service to which I have been appointed. You will never know how much your welcome this evening means to me.

———

I deem it an honor that I have been asked to respond to your words of welcome. True, our years of active leadership as Matrons and Patrons are over but never for one moment have we given up our interest. We are ever jealous of the Chapter's good works and stand ready—as we always have—

to give the benefit of our experience whenever it has been requested. We look forward to this night each year. It is "our party" and we would feel cheated if we were not permitted once more to greet you and thank you for all you have been to us, and still are. No Worthy Matron or Worthy Patron can ever say at the end of his year that the task is over. Rather does it seem that "once a Worthy Matron or Worthy Patron, always a Worthy Matron or Worthy Patron." You are still "our baby" and we have watched you grow in numbers and service with great joy. We shall always stand ready to do what we can to help. We thank you most heartily for your loving welcome. It is truly heart warming. When we enter the Chapter room your happy smiles and kindly words are indeed a welcome home.

———

Words cannot express how much I thank you. The spontaneous warmth of your welcome has made me feel not only that I am among friends but that I am "at home."

———

III

INCOMING MATRON'S RESPONSES AND ADDRESSES

I THANK you for the honor and confidence that you have shown in advancing me to the East and entrusting to my care for the coming year the leadership of this Chapter. My heart thrills with pride and I shall do my utmost to prove that your trust has not been misplaced.

———

In accepting this high office I fully realize the heavy responsibility that goes with it. In assuming the duties of this position I accept the token of your confidence as a sacred trust and pledge to give you my best efforts for the welfare of our Order.

———

I wish to express my deep appreciation and gratitude for the honor that has been conferred upon me. I assure you that I shall earnestly endeavor to merit your confidence and trust. While no organization can entirely rise above its leadership it is equally true that no leadership can become truly effective without complete cooperation, and I ask your whole-hearted assistance in our work for our beloved Chapter.

———

By the grace of God and the favor of you, my Sisters and Brothers, I stand tonight as the Worthy Matron of this Chapter which I have loved so well for so many years. You have placed in my hands a sacred trust. Every day of this coming year I shall guard that trust and give the best that is within me to promote the welfare of this Chapter. For the honor you have conferred upon me I thank you with a grateful heart.

———

There are times when one cannot express in words what is in the heart. You have chosen me to be your Matron and to be thus honored makes me proud, yet humble. I sincerely thank you for this expression of your confidence. My one wish is that I may be true and faithful in all my undertakings. I pledge to do my best and hope I may measure up in some degree to the expectations of you whom I serve.

No man lives unto himself alone—and no Chapter can give its best service unless all its members join in promoting its best interests. We may not move mountains but if we do the work that falls to us and do it to the best of our ability, we may rest in the consciousness of work well done.

Even with the best of intentions no Worthy Matron can be of full use to her Chapter unless she has behind her the respect, confidence and, above all, the cooperation of the Chapter. The fact that you have placed me in the East shows that you have given me the first two and I ask for the last in the full assurance that it will be given me. Alone I can do little— together we can make of ——— Chapter a force for good in the community.

May God's blessing follow us in all we do and may we receive courage, wisdom and strength to carry on our task from day to day.

———

Tonight you have given me great joy and happiness in installing me as your Worthy Matron for the coming year. I will strive to the best of my ability to be worthy of the high honor conferred upon me. I pledge my time, loyalty and efforts to our Order. No one person can carry on the work of the Chapter alone and I ask the support and cooperation of each and every one of you. The past is beyond recall but a new year is before us and if we all work together we shall have a happy and successful year.

―――――

A new Chapter year has begun and while I am very grateful for the confidence reposed in me I am not unmindful of the tremendous responsibilities that come with the acceptance of the office. It is a privilege for me to work with you and I shall try to perform each duty, great or small, with faithfulness and impartiality. Not only do I ask your cooperation but also your patience and understanding. I pledge you the very best of my mind, heart and energy, and ask that you covenant with me in a motto worthy of our principles which may be summed up in these words: In large things, *unity;* in lesser things, *tolerance;* in all things, *charity.* A leader must serve a people. One person alone can make only a trail; the broad highway is beaten out by many marching feet. The next year is ours—to advance or to go backward. Sometimes we fail to comprehend the mighty opportunities that face us but we can understand enough to realize that if we will but pull together we can place our Order nearer its God-given destiny.

―――――

It is a great privilege to be your Worthy Matron, but one that carries with it a great duty, a duty I owe as much to God, my country, my neighbor and myself as to my Chapter. I accept this honorable duty with a truly humble spirit and a desire to be supremely useful. Tonight I am more deeply conscious of the confidence you have reposed in me than ever before. May God ever guide me as I endeavor to fulfill the responsible trust you have committed to me.

———

I desire to express my deep appreciation for bestowing upon me the greatest honor within your power and promise that I will serve you to the best of my ability. I thank you for your loyalty. May we follow the light of our Star in the East and become a leading power for good in our community.

———

You will not be in the chair in the East but I know you will be sitting on the sidelines ready to give your able support and assistance. Those of us who are waiting to attain the farthest point of our Star will profit greatly by your help, experience and advice, as well as just knowing that you are there to help when needed.

———

IV

TRIBUTES TO RETIRING WORTHY MATRON

THE greatest satisfaction that can come into one's life is the knowledge of duties well performed and of having lived according to high principles and lofty ideals. This satisfaction is surely yours tonight. Unselfishly and lovingly, with a heart that was always kind and true, you have given us your best. We have appreciated you and felt throughout the year that your example was a guiding star.

> As you lay down your gavel,
> Oh, Worthy Matron dear,
> You leave behind you happiness,
> Good fellowship and cheer.

> You've paved the way with kindness,
> With loyalty and truth;
> You've always been most faithful—
> A loyal friend, forsooth.

> You've paved a road of peacefulness,
> Of friendships most sincere.
> In our garden of sweet memories
> 'Twill live year after year.

———

We are not unmindful of the many sacrifices you have made for our Chapter. We are indeed most grateful for the inspira-

14

tion you have shown in leading our Chapter on to greater heights and nobler deeds.

————

We know that every task performed, whether great or small, was always gladly done. In the field of service for the Chapter you are excelled by none.

————

We appreciate your unfaltering devotion to our Chapter. The zeal you have shown for our beautiful Order and your willingness to be of service have impressed us all. If it were not for your faith and devotion we would not have been able to carry on to a successful conclusion our program for the year.

————

A year ago you took your station in the East. One year—twelve long months—and yet, to us, how short the time has seemed. Under your guidance our Chapter has been happy, busy and a real help to many. You have met the problems that confronted you with courage and determination and have solved them in a way most satisfactory to us all. We feel that you have always had the good of the Chapter at heart and know you have striven to give it of your best.

————

V

TRIBUTES TO RETIRING WORTHY MATRON WITH PRESENTATION OF GIFT

THE ancient custom handed down from the Romans of sealing friendship with a gift of flowers is often followed in our Order. Hence we offer you these roses; may their fragrance bring you the message of true friendship.

———

As you review the year just past you will find much to treasure in your memory. We, as your officers, will always cherish this year of service under your guidance—a year that has brought us a better appreciation of your kindness, helpfulness and loving thought for others. It is hard to put into words all that we feel for you and so we ask you to let this small gift speak for us—not only tonight, but always.

———

Accept this small gift. It comes to you not only as an expression of our love but also of our appreciation of the hard work, loving thought and unselfish endeavor that have marked your year as Matron. ——— Chapter will ever remember you with love and gratitude.

———

The gift without the giver is bare.
We hope you will plainly see
Through the "eye of your heart" that this little gift
Is decked out like a Christmas tree!

———

As you enter the ranks of Past Matrons may you have nothing but pleasant memories. As a tangible evidence of our regard for you we ask that you accept this small gift. The love and best wishes of the Chapter go with it and will follow you always.

———

Accept this small gift with love from us all; but we ask that this night bring you a greater gift than this. May the secret of its gladness fill your heart; may the warmth behind the good fellowship, the love in the friendly smile, and the good will of all be yours, not only tonight but always. These are truly gifts worth while.

———

I hold in my arms—rosebuds, a rose for every year of your devoted service to our beautiful Eastern Star. These roses will fade and wither; their leaves will drop away and their fragrance be but a memory. But the blossoms of our affection for you will ever bloom in the gardens of our hearts and their fragrance will ever be yours as the years come and go.

———

There is an old adage to the effect that actions speak louder than words. Your service to the Chapter this year has been shouted from the housetops and as a small token of appreciation for all your hard work and loving care we ask you to accept this small package—a true love gift.

———

In behalf of your ————— Committee, I wish to assure you that it has been a genuine pleasure to serve you in our small way. We have endeavored to make this occasion a fitting climax to your successful year with its many happy events and we assure you that your kind words of appreciation have more than repaid us for all our efforts.

> For sweet as a rose art thou,
> So lovely, constant and true;
> We gather up all our flowers
> And pass them on to you.

How often have we seen the slogan "Say it with flowers." From time immemorial the rose has oeen a symbol of love and so tonight we ask you to accept this bouquet of roses with all our love and best wishes that joy and happiness will follow you all your days.

Presentation of jewel:

During the past year I have had a great many pleasant experiences but I can assure you it is not one of the least to present to you this Worthy Matron's jewel.

To be the Worthy Matron of a Chapter is not an easy job; it means a lot of hard work, untiring effort and unstinted giving of time and energy. To the unthinking of us who sit in Chapter and see you calm and smiling in the East, being a Worthy Matron doesn't seem to be such a hard task. Only those of us who know how the good of the Order and continued well being of the Chapter have been in your mind and heart, and how you have striven for both, can realize how great must be your satisfaction, now that your year as leader is ended, to know that something attempted, something done, has earned for you some small measure of repose.

We ask you to accept this jewel, not as a recompense for services rendered, but as a memento of our love, thanks and appreciation for all you have done for our Chapter this year.

VI

RETIRING WORTHY MATRON'S RESPONSES
AND ADDRESSES

AND now we have come to the end of the year. To me it has been such a happy year—a year that has left memories that time cannot dim. It has given me friends whose love shall live on and on. I acknowledge with sincere gratitude each and every kindness shown me. Life will be more rich and complete because of this year of service to, and with, you.

I sincerely thank you for the confidence that was reposed in me when you placed in my hands the welfare of the Chapter. I can assure you that I have tried zealously to guard its every interest and have endeavored throughout the year to serve the Chapter solely through a most profound sense of love and duty.

I am grateful for all your kindnesses to me. The friendships made and experiences gained are mine forever. As I lay down my responsibility to our Chapter I have the satisfaction of knowing that I have ever been faithful to my trust.

I thank you for the privilege of serving you and for the many courtesies shown me. The trust and confidence you have placed in me have been greatly appreciated. I have striven at all times to give of my best to the Chapter and hope that I may be judged, not by what I have done, but by what I have tried to do.

———

I wish today that you could know my heart, but words cannot always voice our deepest emotions. They are but the spoken symbols of our thoughts and mine are indeed insufficient to express my gratitude for your love, loyalty, kindness and devoted cooperation throughout the year.

———

Have you ever stood at the foot of a high hill and seen the road winding up to the top? How steep it looked, how long, how hard to climb. But as you traveled upward it seemed to straighten out and you got to the top thinking it wasn't such a hard road after all.

Such has been my experience this past year. When I took office as your Worthy Matron it was with trepidation in my heart but a determination to give my best to our beloved Chapter and so to work from day to day that at the end of the year I might hear you say "Well done, good and faithful servant." And now I find that most of my fears were imaginary. You were all so kind and helpful and did so much to ease my load that tonight, as I stand at the top of my hill, I can look back and truly wonder why I thought it would be so hard. Never can I thank you enough for all your help and encouragement.

Brother ————, I was most happy to have you in the East with me. I looked to you at all times for advice and assistance and never did you fail me.

And my official family—you were just that; standing together and working always for the good of the Order, thinking not of yourselves but of the Chapter and doing cheerfully and with a smile all the tasks that came your way. Without you I never could have done my part. Words cannot express how much I thank you.

May I leave with you this wish: That the happiest day of the past year be as the saddest of the year to come; that success, joy and happiness may ever follow you; that the Star in the East ever light your pathway; and that "The Lord watch between me and thee while we are absent, one from the other."

I wish I knew some special way—
That I could just begin
To say how I appreciate
How nice you all have been.
But since you know me pretty well
And know my feelings, too,
You know how happy are the thoughts
That prompt this wish for you:
May God bless each and all of you.

You have been ever faithful. How largely the success of this year belongs to you! Accept my sincere appreciation and gratitude for your loyalty and help.

I shall never cease to be grateful for the privilege of serving you. I have held my office as a sacred trust, and as I relinquish it, it is with the wish that I may continue to serve in any way that may be asked of me. I assure you that my interest will ever continue.

Twilight falls; my year is ended;
Gone the sun's revealing light;
Lines of earth and sky are blended;
Softly, gently, comes the night.

"And may the Lord watch between me and thee, while we are absent one from the other."

My sincerest thanks are given for the help and confidence shown me. I asked for your loyalty and cooperation and have been given them to the fullest. Words seem inadequate to express my appreciation and thanks to you for all the many, many things you have done for me. The busy, happy hours I have spent with and for you will ever remain in my memory.

I deeply appreciate every confidence you have placed in me and the pleasures we have enjoyed together this year. Your cooperation and loyalty have been the inspiration that every Worthy Matron needs in order to give her best service.

To Worthy Patron:

It has been a pleasure to serve with you because you expressed at all times such a vital interest in all the affairs of the Chapter and responded most willingly to all requests.

Happy am I that you shared the East with me. In every particular you have measured up to what a Patron should be. You have responded promptly to every call I have made upon you. Your wise counsel, splendid advice, encouragement and sympathetic understanding have meant much. If the

year claims any measure of success, we share the honor together.

———

A last tribute to my Worthy Patron, who stood so faithfully
by my side guiding me by advice and counsel. You have known
the many difficulties that I encountered and have given much
to make our year a success. I trust this year of years will
ever remain one of the brightest pages in your book of
memory. As the curtain is lowered upon our administration,
may life bring to you in abundant measure all joy and happiness.

———

To Chaplain:

You have shared the joys of the year with me and have
been a real tower of strength and help. May God hold you
ever in His keeping.

———

To Associate Matron:

Your friendship, kindness and encouragement have been an
inspiration to me. Very soon I shall deliver the emblem of
authority into your hands. My sincere wish for you is a
successful year and that you may receive the same hearty
support and cooperation from the members of the Chapter
that have been mine. May your year be crowned with the greatest success.

> A year of good fortune I'm wishing for you—
> A year of achievement—of dreams coming true;
> A year full of happiness, health and content;
> In fact, the best year you ever have spent.

———

Your help and never failing interest will never be forgotten and for your loyal service I thank you most sincerely. In a few hours the mantle of authority will fall upon your shoulders and I pledge to you my heartiest support. May our Order grow and flourish under your guidance and may the year that awaits you at tomorrow's rise of sun be one of fruitful service to our Chapter—may it be a year of dreams come true.

To Incoming Worthy Matron:

To you, Sister ————, who are to take my place, I give my sincerest best wishes and hope you may have as happy a year as mine has been. I know you will receive from the Chapter the same whole-hearted support that has been given me. If I can help make your task easier, your burden lighter, I shall deem it a great privilege. I am sure the whole Chapter joins me in the desire to make your year one of the happiest you have ever known.

May the year of honor coming to you
Be one of achievement—of dreams come true.
May its quota of happiness, health and content
Make it quite the best year you ever have spent.
May each eventide bring you a mind free from care
And a heart full of courage to do and to dare.

I wish for you health, joy and happiness. May the coming year be one of fulfillment; may it bind us ever closer and keep us the friends we are now

For I know you and you know me
As each one knows himself to be.
We meet each other face to face
And see therein a truer grace.
Life has so many hidden woes—
So many thorns for every rose—
But the soul of .things our hearts can see,
'Cause I know you, and you know me.

———

To Officers:

I want to thank each and every one of you for your many kindnesses during the year. My work with you has been a pleasure and I really feel that you are the finest officers any Matron ever had. Your eagerness and willingness to assist me in every way have proved your worth, and the memory of your friendship and sincere cooperation will be a part of a lovely garden all my own—

For I have a garden where rare flowers grow—
Flowers no other garden may know:
Friendship, faith and loyalty true
That bloom in my heart for friends like you.

———

To Musicians:

God sent his singers upon the earth
With songs of gladness and of mirth
That they might touch the hearts of men
And bring them back to heaven again.

Music is an inspiration, the one art that is understood by rich and poor alike. My sincere thanks for all the beauty you have added to our meetings through your lovely music.

———

I like to think of music as a wondrous link with God. It sometimes takes the place of prayer. When we are bowed down under a burden of care, and words fail us, music, having no country, creed or race, can give to each according to his need. I have gained inspiration and help through your beautiful music. Our meetings would have lost a goodly part of their solemnity and dignity without your service.

———

VII

WORTHY PATRON'S ACCEPTANCE AND RETIRING ADDRESSES

WE Masonic members of the Eastern Star appreciate fully the faith, courage and determination of our Chapter in following out the precepts of the Order. We are in full accord with your ambitions but too often we sit back and say to ourselves "Oh, that is the women's work. Let them do it." However, there comes to some of us the time when the question is put to us fairly—"Will *you* do *your* part to help the Chapter carry out its program and take its rightful place in the community?" We may pull a little false modesty stunt and pooh-pooh the idea of our being any good as a Worthy Patron but, just the same, we almost burst with pride to think you have considered us good enough to sit in the East with the Worthy Matron.

I most humbly accept the honor you have shown me. I shall count it not only a duty but a privilege to be of such help as I can in guiding the Chapter through the coming year. They say "two heads are better than one," and I hope that when Sister ————— and I get our heads together something good will be forthcoming.

In all sincerity I thank you for the confidence you have shown in me in asking me to be your Worthy Patron for the coming year, and assure you that anything that I can do I shall do with all my might, that you may never regret your choice.

———

Tonight you have conferred upon me the honor of being your Patron. I thank you most sincerely. Just to say a simple "thank you" seems too small, but I hope to show, through my year's service, my devotion to the Chapter. I shall strive to deserve the confidence you have placed in me. I ask the co-operation and good will of each individual member to help make this next year a most successful one for the Chapter.

———

Many of you, no doubt, have heard the story of the hungry bear that entered a pioneer cabin and was killed, after great exertion, by the woman of the house while her husband hid ingloriously behind the door. But after the tumult and the shouting had died he went around bragging about how they had killed a bear. "Me and Betty, *we* did it." Well, after some fashion that is what happened this year. "Me and Betty" did the best for you we knew how—and I want to tell you right now that I wasn't behind the door *all* the time!

When you asked me to serve as your Patron I accepted the honor knowing that it would mean much work but also much pleasure. Sister ——— wasted no time; she had her campaign laid out and, like a good general, had us all doing our proper job. She had us working! We hope the result of our labors has been satisfactory to you. We have striven to make this year one of the best the Chapter has ever had. Now we rest from our labors, and if you are pleased we shall be satisfied. We may not have done all that we hoped to do but what we have accomplished has always been with the good of the Chapter in mind.

To Brother ———, who comes after me, I can only say that he has ahead of him a year of service that will make him very proud to be a member of the Eastern Star. May he enjoy his year as much as I have mine.

———

Your Worthy Matron and I have endeavored to make the past year of service an uplifting one to the Chapter and have met with a warm response, for which we are most grateful. We feel that the work in the coming year will be carried on in the same spirit—that our work will be earnest and our play enjoyable, that it may be profitable to each and every one individually and to the Chapter in general and leave in the community cause only for admiration and respect.

———

VIII

TRIBUTES TO THE BIBLE—BIBLE PRESENTATIONS

THE Bible is ·God's gift to mankind. Within its covers lie the secrets of how to live and how to die. Upon its teachings our beloved Order of the Eastern Star is founded. It must always be open upon our altar in order to give authority to all the work of the Chapter.

———

No Chapter of the Order of the Eastern Star can be opened or transact business unless the open Bible rests upon its altar. Is this a mere form or does it really mean something?

Our Order is founded on, and built around, a belief in God. Every member of the Order, before being admitted, must answer in the affirmative the question, "Do you believe in the existence of a Supreme Being?"

In the Ten Commandments, received by Moses direct from God, we find the fundamental basis of all moral conduct. The Son of God Himself gave us that greatest and most complete of all commandments that we love our neighbor as ourself. Here is all the philosophy and guidance needed for a perfect life.

Out of these sacred pages come the heroines of our Order. Each one brings us a lesson, yes, more than a lesson—a direct admonition from the Word of God.

Thus through our original declaration of belief in a Supreme Being and the lessons of our Star the Bible becomes the very living heart of our Order. In placing it on our altar we renew our faith in, and allegiance to, God. Like the Shekinah, it is the symbol of the very presence of God among us. As such, we place it on our altar and hold it in utmost reverence.

—*James A. Gibson*

———

The Bible is a living Book. It has lived through centuries of criticism and has not been superseded; the Psalms of David still comfort wounded hearts. The teachings of Christ will never be outgrown; untold millions of aching hearts have been comforted by His words. In trial and tribulation, sickness and sorrow, the loyal heart always turns to Him, and never turns in vain. It is the traveler's map, the pilgrim's staff, the pilot's compass, the soldier's sword and the Christian's character.

I now give this Book to you. Read it to be wise; believe it to be safe; practice it to be holy. Study this Book; live by its precepts; follow its light that shines upon your pathway so that when you come to the end of the way you may leave behind you an influence that will cause those you leave behind to rise up and call you blessed.

———

I now present to you this Holy Bible upon which you took the solemn obligation of our Order. It is yours—to read, to study, to treasure. We ask you to remember that

> We search the world for truth; we cull
> The good, the true, the beautiful
> From all old flower-fields of the soul;
> And, wearied seekers of the best,
> We come back, laden from the quest,
> To find that all the sages said
> Is in the Book our mothers read.

Its cover is white, signifying innocence, and is to remind you of that purity of life and conduct which should be the aim of every member of our Order. Within its pages you will find the stories you have heard tonight. There also you may read of the Star of the East that guided the Wise Men of old and which today will safely guide our faltering footsteps through the labyrinth of life.

———

IX

MOTHER

GOD could not be everywhere, so He made mothers.

―――

Blessed are the mothers of yesterday, for their mercies shall be called beautiful and beneficent. They are like flowers growing by sunken gardens, beside still waters, and in green fields.

Blessed are the mothers of today, for they have the keeping of tomorrow in their hands and in their hearts, and the destiny of hearts, of homes and of nations.

―――

Sometimes my humbleness takes flight
And leaves me courting sophistry,
And worldly pride bedims my sight
Of God and life's great mystery.

And then I see a mother's eyes
Upon her babe, her crooning hear.
"Oh, God," my heart, repentant, cries,
"Who could be proud, with Thee so near?"

―J. A. Glidewell.

―――

If I could concentrate all the fragrance of the world into one flower, I would call it a rose. If I could concentrate all the melody of the universe into one composition, I would call

33

it the Messiah. If I could concentrate all the tenderness and sympathy of the world into one endearing term, I would call it MOTHER. No other word in any language is invested with such charm and pathos as this. The depths of the soul are broken up at its sound and the very incense of heaven clings to it.

The word "mother," like music, has charm. All down the ages great men have paid tribute to their mothers. Abraham Lincoln said, "All that I am, or hope to be, I owe to my mother."

Youth fades, love droops, the leaves of friendship fall;
A mother's secret hope outlives them all.

Hundreds of stars in the evening sky,
Hundreds of shells on the shore together,
Hundreds of birds that go singing by,
Hundreds of lambs in the sunny weather,
Hundreds of dewdrops to greet the dawn,
Hundreds of bees in the fragrant clover,
But only one mother the whole world over.

God gave the sun to warm the earth,
And birds and flowers for our delight;
God gave us hills, and winds, and streams,
And stars to guide us through the night.
And then He gave another gift
More precious far than all the others—
To have us know His love for us,
He made and gave us mothers.

Some folks love us when we're good,
Others, when we're bad;
Some folks love us when we're gay,
Others, when we're sad.
It takes some special quality
To win the world's applause,
But mothers are the only ones
Who love us just "because!"

One of the sweetest days we celebrate is Mother's Day, with its cherished memories of her who protected and guided our childhood.

Standing steadfast in calm or storm, casting their light far into the night, are those havens of safety, the lighthouses. Their beams warm the hearts of those at sea for to them they are guiding lights, beacons of safety.

Are not mothers similar to these lighthouses? They stand steadfast in the home in fair and stormy weather. The same love that guided our childish footsteps still serves as a beacon for our later years. No matter where our paths may lead us, mother's light, even though she has been called Home, still shines brightly in our hearts and beckons us to safety.

Our mothers will never be forgotten; their memory will linger after all else has faded. We humbly thank her for being our beacon light through all the storms and calms of life.

We read about the mothers
Of the days of long ago
With their gentle, wrinkled faces
And their hair as white as snow.
They were middle-aged at forty,

And at fifty donned lace caps;
At sixty clung to shoulder shawls,
And loved their little naps.
But I love the modern mother
Who can share in all our joys,
And who understands the problems
Of her growing girls and boys.
She may boast that she is sixty—
But her heart is twenty-three—
My glorious, bright-eyed mother
Who is keeping young with me.

X

IN MEMORIAM

THERE is no death. Earth's raiment laid aside,
The deathless spirit wings its onward flight.
In heavenly realms nothing can us divide;
The veil is rent, it can no longer hide.
And so, dear ones who wait, obedient bide.
Eternal love controls, and all is right.

We are so selfish about death. We count our grief
Far more than we consider their relief
Whom the Great Reaper gathers in his sheaf
No more to know the seasons' constant change;
And we forget that it means only life—
Life with all joy, peace, rest and glory rife,
The victory won and ended all the strife,
And heaven no longer far away, and strange.

Say not their work is done.
No deed of love or kindness ever dies
But in the life of others multiplies.
Say it is just begun.

Our dear ones have only passed into the sunset's glow,
leaving precious memories that nothing can take away.

Thus star by star declines
  'Til all have passed away,
As morning higher climbs
  To pure and perfect day.
They have not gone to far off lands
  But to "that house not made with hands."

———

God calls our loved ones, but we lose not wholly
  What He has given.
They live on earth in thought and deed as truly
  As in His heaven.

———

Somewhere back of the sunset,
Where loveliness never dies,
She lives in a land of glory
'Mid the blue and gold of the skies.

And we, who have known and loved her
Whose passing has brought sad tears,
Will cherish her memory always
To brighten the passing years.

———

It is only our faith in God's promises that comforts our sad hearts in the face of death. It is the voice of faith that whispers low:

Our times are in His hand
Who saith, "A whole I planned;
Trust God; see all, nor be afraid.

———

What seem to us but sad, funereal tapers
May be heaven's distant lamps.

———

It is hard to fill the vacancy that the Grim Reaper leaves but we must realize that death enters every household, and sometime we will understand.

A tender thought we bring to those
Who mourn o'er a vacant chair—
We know and feel that our Lord knows best,
And our loved ones we'll meet over there.

————

To continue down the pathway of life without our loved one at our side is truly hard; it seems as though the whole world has collapsed and the way that once looked bright and cheery suddenly appears dark and gloomy; but the same heavenly Father who sends His comforting love to each of us will give to our Sister strength to continue, secure in the knowledge that "death is but the beginning of life."

————

He is not dead, this friend of our affection,
But gone on to that school
Where he no longer needs our kind protection
And God Himself doth rule.

————

The voice that we loved is silent now
And stilled is the helpful hand,
But we know that God will use them both
In that wonderful, heavenly land.
Though we say "she is dead," she still lives on
In memories tender and true,
And the cadence of her voice still rings
Our faith and hope to renew.

————

Sisters and Brothers: We have gathered here today to pay loving tribute to the memory of our dear Sister ————, and as a token of affection to her memory, I place this floral wreath, a tribute of our faithful love.

> Not broken ties, but just a veil between
> Our earthly vision and that world unseen;
> A little time to wait while loved ones there
> Keep tender watch until we, too, may share
> The perfect peace of God, the perfect love
> That's known to those who dwell with Him above.

————

Sisters and Brothers: I come to this altar, dear to the hearts of all who have learned the lessons of our Order, to pay tribute to our associates who have passed into the glory and understanding of the Eternal. No longer may we consult with them about our temporal affairs and problems. They have gone from us and from the petty trials of life. We know they shall not return but that we shall go to them. Happy in this glorious belief we perform this ceremony, not in sorrow but in loving remembrance of our association with those who have gone on before to welcome us to our Eternal Home.

> As our tribute thus we pay
> To those we love who might not stay,
> Through pearly gates, once more ajar,
> We send the greeting from our Star.
> We know the parting is not long.
> We, too, shall join the silent throng.
> God closed their eyes to mortal sight
> And tenderly we say, "Good night."

[At the close of the tribute a spray of white lilies is placed on the altar.]

————

They are waiting for us in the City of Peace,
And whithersoever we fare
We shall ne'er find a pathway that leads not at last
With unerring certainty there.
They are waiting for us; we are hastening on.
Each eventide brings us more near
The shadowy portals through which have gone
Those we miss on our journeying here.

———

She has seen the sunrise with the Master—
Has seen the rose-bright morning all aglow.
She has touched the tender leaves of healing,
And lingers where the clear blue waters flow.

She has heard the golden bells and their soft ringing;
Beheld the sunlit towers of heaven so bright;
With Him she walks in heaven's fairest gardens
Where are ferns so green, and tender lilies white.

She has seen the sunrise with the Master.
Earth's long and weary night has passed away,
All her pain and earthly cares have been forgotten
In that land of quiet joy and endless day.

———

I know not the way I am going
But well do I know my Guide.
With a child-like trust I give my hand
To the loving Friend at my side.
And the only thing I say to Him
As he takes it, is "Hold it fast.
Suffer me not to lose my way
But bring me home at last."

———

At last night shall fall. The things that now seem so important shall all be left behind and the Master's voice shall be heard saying: "The day is done; the work is finished; lay down the tools, it will soon be time to go to sleep." If in that hour we can remember that in our life's journey we have tried to do our part—that when the sun was withering we have not shirked our stint; that when another has grown weary we have tried to speak a word of hope, and lend a hand that would help and never hinder; if in our work we have known how to sing and taught others to sing; if we know that in our hearts we have cherished hatred towards no human being but have tried to forgive as we would wish to be forgiven, and to judge charitably the failures of others as we would want them to judge of ours; then, whatever mistakes we may have made, we can lie down as peacefully as a little child at evening, who, with his mother's hand on his, passes into slumber knowing that all is well; sure that there is One watching beside us who "neither slumbers nor sleeps," and that when we shall awaken it will be to find ourselves in the Old Home, surrounded by those whom we have loved—and that it will be morning.

God rest his gallant spirit; give him peace
And crown his brow with amaranth; and set
The saintly palm branch in his able hand
Amid the conquering armies of the skies.

"He giveth His beloved sleep."

They are not dead, those loved ones who have passed
Beyond our vision for a little while;
They have but reached the light, while we still grope
In darkness where we cannot see them smile.

Somewhere there is life eternal;
Somewhere there's a home above;
There's no night without a dawning;
Beyond this death is God, and love.

The earth is poorer since they took their flight,
But heaven is richer now that they are there;
And on their brows gleam with transcendent light
Such crowns as honest, upright ones shall wear.

He has stamped on the margin of Life broad and brave
The good which he wrought and the love which he gave;
And the path of his kindness is plainer today
Than the name which is graved on a tablet of gray.

The chain of fraternal friendship
Is made of links of gold
Which we fondly hold and cherish—
Our friends, both new and old.
Then, one by one, they sever,
Just why we cannot tell,
But we trust the heavenly Father
Who doeth all things well.

Into the field the Reaper came,
Calling these lovely flowers by name;
Each bowed its head in submissive grace
And naught of fear bore they a trace.
Jesus the Christ hath shown the way
And they have followed, steadfastly.

Above the cross His Star doth shine,
Emblem of truth and life divine.
Triumphant now, enrolled on high
Their spirits live. They did not die.

———

To a beautiful garden these friends have gone—
  To the land of perfect rest.
Their work is done, and the setting sun
  Has sealed their life's long quest.
They have left this earthly garden
  For a home beyond the sea.
Though they are gone, they still live on
  In the garden of memory.

———

Sleep on, dear friends, such lives as thine
  Have not been lived in vain,
But shed an influence rare, divine,
  On those that here remain.

———

When Death draws down the curtain of the night
And those we love in its deep darkness hide,
We can but wait the coming of the light
And bless the memories that still abide.

———

XI

MASONRY AND THE EASTERN STAR

HAND in hand these Orders shall go
Along life's toilsome road,
Both lending aid to weary ones
Who falter 'neath their load;
Both giving help to pilgrims weak
When traveling from afar;
The one by Compasses led straight,
The other following the Star.

The relationship of the Eastern Star to Freemasonry is closely coordinated for the betterment and increased happiness of mankind. From its inception, the Star has had an impelling religious appeal which, with its actual service, has brought it to a position that justifies perpetuity.

The Order of the Eastern Star and the Masonic Fraternity, always so much alike in their fundamental principles and aims, understand each other just a little better than before. This, in itself, is a happy accomplishment. We should have a better understanding of each other's hopes and aspirations. We should take inventory of our separate abilities and correlate our aims to the advantage of both. Thus we strengthen ourselves and our position in our respective communities. In doing this we will be following Christ and adding strength to the moral forces of our separate constituencies. That this is the hope and prayer of us all there can be no doubt. May this be a year of outstanding service and advancement.

————

Address by A Freemason:

In this day and age when the world is filled with propaganda regarding various philosophies and theories it is desirable that men and women have some sort of an organization in which to unite to teach right thinking and right living. We have that type of institution in the Masonic Fraternity and in the Order of the Eastern Star.

Perhaps some of you would like to be let in on a little Masonic secret. You notice the carpet you have on your floor is a five pointed star. The carpet we have in the Blue Lodge is a pentagon, teaching identically the same principles that you teach in the Order of the Eastern Star. Let me tell you what I consider the foundation upon which the Order of the Eastern Star and the Masonic Fraternity are builded:

Using either the five points of the star or the pentagon as the basic structure, we have five sturdy pillars which we may denominate temperance, fortitude, prudence and brotherly love. Resting upon these pillars and extending from one to the other we find heavy joists—fidelity, constancy, loyalty, faith and love. Running from these corner posts to the mass of center pillars we find courage, penitence, perseverence, steadfastness and patience, all bound together by three solid cables —faith, hope and charity.

A superstructure that is erected upon that type of foundation necessarily must be all harmony, beauty and strength of purpose. This superstructure is composed of the characters of

Freemasons and members of the Order of the Eastern Star, and it is up to us, as individual members, to so weave into our lives these various virtues I have mentioned, and which are a part of our institution, that we may not be guilty of doing anything except that which will make this world better, and that we may continue to teach the cardinal principles of the fatherhood of God, the brotherhood of man, the resurrection of the body and the immortality of the soul.

It has been said that fraternal organizations such as ours were what the Savior had in mind when He commanded His disciples to go to the ends of the earth and teach the gospel of brotherly love. We honor the Masonic Order for the splendid work they are doing and we also find avenues of usefulness along the same lines. We aid the widow and orphan; we visit the sick; we alleviate the distress of our unfortunate members and find great joy in spreading happiness and giving service.

What we need most today—what all Eastern Stars and Masons are striving to bring about—is to practice more zealously the lessons we teach so that the brotherhood of man, peace, fraternal love and the Golden Rule will become realities. We should go hand in hand; no one goes his way alone. All that we put into the lives of others comes back again into our own.

The Masonic Fraternity is an organization endeavoring to plant in the lives of men the wonderful things for which Masonry stands.

The Order of the Eastern Star appeals to the lives of thinking men and women. It is not to be considered just a woman's organization, as some seem to think it is. Both men and women are giving their best service to our great Order and it should bring out the best we have in us.

Why shouldn't we be proud of our beloved Order and give our best to it? It molds real character and is far reaching in influence. It has a building program that should appeal to the thoughtful; and there always has been a place for loyal men and women in such a system.

May we, as members of these two great organizations, make a lasting contribution to the welfare of mankind by studying, thinking, and living "Peace on earth, good-will to men."

—*Daisy M. Crist.*

The Order of the Eastern Star has a spiritual appeal to all, like the ideals of Masonry, that will always continue. It is more than a sisterhood and brotherhood, more than a system of ritualism, or a field for social enjoyment. It is religious, though not a religion. All its lessons are based on Biblical history and are for the betterment and enlightenment of humanity.

It was a realization of the religious good that might be accomplished that moved Rob Morris and Robert Macoy to bring to life the impressive ritual of the Eastern Star—a ritual virtually the same today as when it was finally completed and adopted in 1868. Their idea in promoting the Eastern Star was that the influence brought about by bringing women into closer relationship with Masonry would bring its performance nearer to its profession—practicing what they preach.

The spirit of cooperation existing between the Masonic Fraternity and the Order of the Eastern Star is most pleasing. Our Order owes its hopes for the future and its accomplishments of the past to the Masonic Order; and we freely acknowledge our debt. We, as members of the Eastern Star, are ever willing and ready to lend all possible assistance to this magnificent Order. We trust that as the years go by this same splendid cooperation and friendliness will continue.

The Masonic Order was first organized for the purpose of protecting the life, liberty and happiness of mankind. The Order of the Eastern Star was later organized to assist Masonry in these fundamental purposes. The world is crying out to us in these days of great suffering and danger. We must not fail to answer the call. Nothing good survives without effort. This has always been true. We must answer the challenge or peril our very existence.

XII

NEW YEARS—EASTER—THANKSGIVING— CHRISTMAS

New Years:

A bright New Year and a sunny track
Along your upward way,
And a song of praise on looking back
When the year has passed away,
And golden sheaves, nor small nor few!
This is our New Years wish for you.

———

We stand upon the threshold of a New Year laden with high hopes for the dominance of that spirit of morals, religion and fraternalism which alone will save our Christian civilization. Never before in the history of the world has there been a greater need for loyalty to the Christian religion. We are not alone; millions who have been compelled to renounce their faith are appealing to us from the "blackout" which is their only hope of safety in these days of war and utter desolation.

We cannot face these truths without asking ourselves how best we can bear our torches into the New Year. Let us go forward into the coming year with these high resolves: To live loyally, to show kindness, to be charitable. Empty words are not enough. Let us put into practice our sacred obligation taken at our altars and help our Sisters and Brothers wherever there is need of aid, comfort and relief; let us put a little more effort into spreading the gospel of cheer; let us waste no time or money on personal pleasures while there is so much constructive work to be done; let us be more willing to share with others those precious things of life which we have considered our personal heritage. We must bear our torches so high that they will reach out into the dark places to show to the Christian world that the Light still burns.

> The year is closed, the record made,
> The last deed done, the last word said;
> And now, with purpose full and clear,
> Let's turn to greet another year.

The door of time swings wide and we stand on the threshold of a new year. We view the road ahead and realize the need of courage and faith to carry on. Courage we may borrow from our very need but faith must be the light from within to guide us on to victory. If we are to be the masters of our destiny we must think right, for thoughts are the most potent power in the universe. We must clear our thoughts of fear, despair and defeat, and with our eyes on the hills, from whence comes our help, go forth each day secure in the knowledge that God has us in his care.

As we enter this New Year may the teachings of our Order have greater significance than ever before. Let us walk by faith and not by sight, and lean not upon our own understanding but in all our ways acknowledge Him and He will direct our paths.

Another year has passed. What has it brought?
A little deeper and a little wiser thought—
A little truer sympathy of friend to friend—
More earnest striving to a common end?
If this be so, blest was this year, indeed,
And heartily we wish it now Godspeed.

———

As we stand on the threshold of this New Year let us pray
for a spirit of humility and self-effacement, with only the desire to serve and help to usher in the dawn of that long-looked-
for day when war shall cease, and peace, brotherhood and
good will among men shall cover the earth even as the waters
cover the face of the deep.

———

Out of the generous hand of time
We come to take another year,
And each of us, from day to day,
Must write upon its pages clear.
God grant that we shall kindlier be,
Speak less in blame and more in praise,
And by the conduct of our lives
Make this a year of happy days.

———

At Thy feet, our God and Father,
Who has blessed us all our days,
We with grateful hearts would gather
To begin the year with praise;
Praise for light so brightly shining
On our steps from heaven above;
Praise for mercies daily twining
Round us golden cords of love.

———

March 91

Easter:

May this Easter season bring you fulfillment of desires and God's rich blessing.

———

This is the spirit of Eastertide:
Faith in the things we cannot see,
For there is much that God must hide
Away from the eyes of you and me.

Just as we know the flowers of spring
Follow the winter's snow and cold,
So does the resurrection bring
Hope and joy and peace untold.

As springtime sets her golden seal
Upon the earth and makes it new,
So may this Eastertide reveal
The greatest joys of life to you.

———

Easter is the festival observed throughout Christendom in commemoration of the resurrection of our Savior. There is no trace of the Easter festival in the New Testament. The sanctity of special times or places was an idea quite alien to the early Christian mind, which was too profoundly absorbed in the events themselves to think of their external benefits. With the dawn of Easter there comes to the true followers of Him, whose Star is our inspiration, the thought of a spiritual awakening and the hope of a resurrected life—a life everlasting. The essential element in the resurrected life is that which leads to moral excellence. We are raised only as we grow in genuine goodness. May the joyous spirit of Easter remain with us throughout the year and help us to emphasize the lesson of the fifth point of our Star which embodies the new commandment that was given to the world centuries ago—that we love one another.

—*Pearl E. Peabody*

Just as Christ's resurrection came after His crucifixion, so does the message of Easter bring us new hope for greater peace and happiness in a world now suffering from death, disaster and confusion. As Christ came forth victorious from the grave, we must believe that ultimately we shall conquer the problems of the world through His living presence. Even in the face of conditions which prevail today Christ still manifests Himself in the lives of those who are passing from their Garden of Gethsemane into the darkness of death. Men of all nations are defending their homes and countries against destruction. Whether they be following wise or false prophets, civilization is still reaching out in hope and faith that there shall be a more abundant life in days to come. Faith, hope, sacrifice and love are but the evidence of the spirit of Christ, who prayed that we be taught to dwell in the world but be spared from its evils.

Let us have hope, faith and an unwavering confidence that out of this great confusion there will come a victory as great as that of the morning of the resurrection when the great stone was rolled away from the tomb and Christ came forth as the manifestation of the ultimate triumph of life over death.

Winter with its rigor and cold, its frosts and inclement blasts, its tempests and sternness, is an emblem of sorrow, sadness and grief. We are glad when the season ends. With spring comes the Eastertide, essentially a season of joy. Birds sing, trees and plants bring forth leaves and buds, and flowers burst into a profusion of color and beauty. All remind us of Easter and God's blessed promise that after the darkness of death there shall come resurrection and life eternal. Let us look forward to Easter time with new hopes, greater purpose in life, and more faith in God and those who live around us.

Thanksgiving:

Once again time has brought us one of the most beautiful customs that has ever prevailed among any people—Thanksgiving Day. It is with grateful, happy hearts that we approach this period of Thanksgiving. We recognize and gladly own that the will of God is the ultimate secret of all true government, and His goodness and mercy the fountain of all real happiness.

We rejoice that we are a free people; that we have a free press; that we may worship Omnipotent God according to the dictate of our own conscience; that want and fear are kept far from us; and on this Thanksgiving Day our hearts openly proclaim our gratitude for the manifest, varied and countless blessings that our Father has bestowed upon us.

While our hearts are saddened because of the terrible conflict prevailing, and our prayers go up for an early and permanent peace, yet with gratitude that knows no bounds, our souls are lifted up in Thanksgiving to our Father that He has given us this free country, so dearly bought, so hardly won, so dearly loved. May we by every thought, word and deed evince a unity of spirit, service and faith that He may continue to lead us in the paths which we must follow

Truly we are thankful for each other, for the fellowship we enjoy, for the spirit of helpfulness, kindly words and deeds, for our beautiful Order, and for His Star that leads us on into spheres of greater happiness and usefulness.

Thanksgiving time! Our minds go back through the years to that desolate winter when valiant men and courageous women endured hardship, sickness and want, well content that they had won for themselves a place where they might have freedom to worship God. Today we are grown into a mighty nation, holding within itself many races, peoples and religions.

May our devotion to God be no less than theirs who celebrated that first Thanksgiving Day. May we resolve that all our great nation shall come to know the freedom, the discipline, the spirit of love and the desire to help others that following Jesus brings.

May we always know freedom from want, fear, and religious intolerance and have the blessing of a free press. For these things our fathers struggled and died. We, too, must fight to keep our precious heritage.

———

> Thou knowest, Lord,
> My thanks are deep
> For raiment warm,
> And work and sleep,
> And life-sustaining
> Meat and bread.
> But these with which
> The soul is fed
> I could not forfeit:
> Music flowing
> From bird and organ,
> Hill wind blowing,
> The jonquils gold,
> The gleaming gray,
> Laughter, and peace,
> And the slow way

A friend grows dear;
And the surety
Thou wilt not fail
In shepherding me.
            —Elaine V. Evans

———

Christmas:

We thank Thee, Lord, that we may live
In peace and comfort Thou dost give.
We thank Thee that Thy sheltering arms
Protect us from the world's alarms;
That though in foreign climes we roam,
Far from our loved ones and our home,
Thy light shall make our pathway clear,
Remove all shadow, sorrow, fear.

May that bright star the Wise Men saw
All wisdom to it ever draw;
May wisdom, worshiping afar,
Enshrine itself within the Star
With faith and hope and love entwined
To rule the hearts of humankind.
Be that bright Star our beacon guide—
This is our prayer at Christmastime.

———

May our hearts be filled with a sincere and reverent spirit
of love and understanding as we approach this glorious season
of the year when we commemorate the birth of Him Whose
Star we have seen in the East. Let us keep love in our hearts,
for love fulfills His law. Let us remember that promoting the
happiness of others will bring us a great and complete joy.

May the Christmas season and the New Year bring to each and every one of us blessings rich, abounding and eternal.

———

May you have the Gladness of Christmas, which is Hope; the Spirit of Christmas, which is Peace; the Heart of Christmas, which is Love.

———

To the members of the Eastern Star Christmas should be of special significance. May the light of the Star still bring to all of us the joys of Christmastide, and may its beams shine upon the pathway of the New Year to guide us in ways of happiness and paths of peace.

———

Eternal Father, we thank Thee for a faith so high that it can link the far-off pilgrim stars with the cradle of a Little Child. Teach us that no hope vouchsafed to the human soul is too high, too holy, to be fulfilled by Thy love and power. Lift up our hearts this day and make us to know that the world is too small for the soul of its dreams. May we be faithful to Thy Morning Star by which we are led out of phantoms into realities.

Drive back the gray shadows which the years have cast over us and let us see Thy guiding Star and hear a music not of earth. Let not our souls be busy inns that have no room for Thee and Thine, but homes of prayer and praise, ready for Thy welcoming. Make us to know that near us, even in our city, is Christ the Savior, Whom seeking with joy, we shall find. Humbly we offer our Christmas prayer in His name. Amen.

—Joseph Fort Newton

———

When Christmas comes around each year it works its age-old miracle. In some strange and wonderful way the whole world is softened by the sacred influence of the Babe in the manger—and the ideal of the Christ, which is implanted in the hearts of men, takes firmer root at Christmas time.

———

Happy bells of Christmas will soon ring out their joyous song of "Peace on earth, good will to men." May their sweet tones echo in our hearts, bringing peace and joy to each and all. At this joyous season let us think of all who need our help and care and give to them freely in gratitude for His love.

———

Christmas must be kept as a time of giving; and that giving should mean some sacrifice to the giver, some radiance of joy, comfort and hope to the recipient. Christmas comes just before the New Year and the hope, kindness and happiness of the holiday season should spill over into the New Year and get us started off with hearts still warm with love kindled by sympathy for others.

The Prince of Peace, whose coming was heralded by the Star we have seen in the East, and at whose feet the Wise Men laid their gifts, has said: "Inasmuch as ye have done it unto one of the least of these, my brethren, ye have done it unto me." So let us give not only of our abundance but make real sacrifices, remembering the words of our Savior, "It is more blessed to give than to receive." Today we have numberless occasions to exercise the real spirit of Christmas. Let us take full advantage of these opportunities. The Christmas spirit means thoughtfulness for others and manifests itself in attention to those who need our care. Wherever human need is met, be it sorrow, discouragement, weariness, or suffering, there the Christ spirit hovers. Over those who serve in the spirit of Love gleams the Star of Bethlehem, the true ideal upon which our Order is founded.

———

This is the season of the year when our hearts are full of gratitude for the many blessings which we have received. We need Christmas this year more than ever before. We need the strength, encouragement and joy which it brings. We need more of the spirit of brotherhood in every walk of life.

The anniversary of the birth of Christ gives each of us the opportunity of doing some good deed, some act of service for humanity. We may contribute to another's happiness or gladden the heart of one who may be discouraged—the widow, the orphan, the sick or the friendless. Christmas may be a beautiful and sacred time if we do our part in keeping it the enduring, simple and wholesome season it ought to be. Let us not forget the needs of our own local community, in the name of Him who has bestowed upon this great land the priceless gifts of freedom and peace.

> Vainly we offer each ample oblation,
> Vainly with gifts would His favor secure.
> Richer by far is the heart's adoration;
> Dearer to God are the prayers of the poor.

———

The most cherished gift bestowed by the passing year is the memory of the pleasant relations with those with whom we have been privileged to serve. May we carry with us at all times the spirit of love which is the foundation of our organization; may the glorious glow of human kindness kindled in the hearts of mankind on that first Christmas be as strong an influence in our lives as it was two thousand years ago.

It is with hearts full of love that we wish you all a Merry Christmas and health, happiness and prosperity in abundance this New Year.

———

Again we find our path leading to the close of another year with its joys and sorrows, failures and successes. As we think back over the year we may grieve that the record may not be up to the desired standard; then comes the determination to do and bear our share in the world's busy ways and help, at this Christmas season, to bear a part in bringing cheer where sorrow is known, and help and comfort where want and need have left sadness and suffering in their wake. The efforts being made among the members of fraternal organizations to carry out these resolves are certain proof that the teachings of the Master are still leading us on.

———

Down through the ages there comes to us once again the Christmas message of "peace on earth, good will toward men." As members of a great organization that has taken unto itself the emblem of the star we should find in the coming of Christmas an especial significance. The Star of Bethlehem should lead us anew in the paths of wisdom as it did the Wise Men of old. It should kindle in our hearts the spark of faith, the glow of hope and the radiance of charity for all who are in need. When the new year comes and the old one is just a memory may the holy meaning of Christmas—peace and good will —remain as the crowning benediction of each day to come. May our heavenly Father guide us, that we may in every sense be co-workers in the service of humanity.

—Nannie Mai Gilbert

———

Christmas is the grand feast of the year—a feast that has as its object making every heart respond to its fullest to happiness, gratitude and good cheer. Happiness is the true end and aim of life; it is derived from duty well done, from generous acts and from being true to an ideal. The time to be happy is now; the way to be happy is to make others happy and to render all possible service in the cause of human progress. Good cheer is the living expression of happiness.

Doing good is the means to an end; it is the means of communicating happiness to others and makes life worth while. It is the most workable way to bind men and nations together in the bonds of universal peace.

A merry Christmas means a wider distribution of comforts to the needy, an overflow of the good things of life into the channels where they are most needed. May this Christmas bring you greater happiness than ever before, and may you find that happiness in your service to humanity.

———

XIII

FRIENDSHIP

THE word "friendship" conjures up in one's mind mutual love, respect, understanding and sacrifice. We have all heard the saying—"A true friend is one who knows all about you and loves you just the same." In other words, personal failings and foibles do not impress a true friend; such human frailties are obscured by the ardent glow of friendship. A philosopher once said, "Friendship should be kept in a constant state of repair."

If you want a friend, be one yourself. Remember this injunction, for love begets love and hate fosters hate. By the same token, friendship begets friendship. It can be truly said that the best proof we have of a man's success in life is his ability to make friends. How poor indeed must be the lonely man. What a void there must be in a man's life who does not possess the knack of making and keeping friends, once acquired. It is a truism that he alone has lost the art of living who has lost the ability to make friends.

What greater blessings can we have than friends? They come to us in our joy and sorrow, and especially in our time of need, and take our burdens upon themselves, showing by loving word and deed that they will help us in our darkest hours. We do not realize until such a time comes that God gave us riches untold when he gave us friends.

It is not the mighty deeds achieved that make life sweet, but just the little acts of kindness to those we meet.

———

Begin the day with friendliness;
Keep friendly all day long.
Keep in your soul a friendly thought,
In your heart a friendly song.
Have in your mind a word of cheer
For all who come your way
And they will greet you, too, in turn,
And wish you a happy day.
—*Marie Woerheide*

———

The world needs the sunshine of your smiles. While man has no direct control over the elements of wind, rain and clouds, yet he isn't as helpless as he would have himself believe. He can smile—and smiles are man-made sunshine.

———

Robert Louis Stevenson said "So long as we love, we serve. So long as we are loved by others I would almost say we are indispensable; and no man is useless while he has a friend." Let us be friends.

———

Count your garden by the flowers,
Never by the leaves that fall.
Count your day by golden hours;
Don't remember clouds at all.
Count your night by stars, not shadows,
Count your life by smiles, not tears,
And with joy in each tomorrow
Count your age by friends, not years.

———

There is no treasure like the treasure
  Of a faithful friend;
There is no pleasure like the pleasure
  Friendliness can lend.
Fame and riches, other pleasures,
  These may quickly pass away.
Friendship and its golden treasures
  Last forever and a day.

I'd like to be the sort of friend
That you have been to me;
I'd like to be the help that you've
Been always glad to be.
I'd like to mean as much to you
Each minute of the day,
As you have been, old friends of mine,
To me along the way.

And that is why I'm wishing now
That I could but repay
A portion of the gladness you
Have strewn along my way.
And could I have but just one wish,
This only would it be:
I'd like to be the sort of friend
That you have been to me.
              —*L. H. Fear*

To understand and to be understood; to be frank, honest,
loving and loyal through good and evil report; comforting
when comfort is needed; rejoicing in another's success and

happiness and sharing one's own success and happiness with another; having an ever broadening love for that which is good and true—such is my conception of an ideal friendship. Such friendship has perceived the real individual as the reflection of God and can never lose sight of the true and real self, however much the clouds of sense may seek to darken the spiritual vision.

> Life is sweet because of the friends we have made
> And the things which in common we share.
> We want to live on, not because of ourselves,
> But because of the people who care.
> It is giving and doing for somebody else
> On which all life's splendor depends
> And the joy of this life, when you've summed it all up,
> Is found in the making of friends.

True friendship is ever fine and beautiful but it is not accomplished with handshaking. There must be an exchange of something warm and sweet, something that will enrich the heart with happiness. There must be some service, no matter how small, that will endure.

Knowing many people does not necessarily mean having many friends. True friendship is not based upon how many people we can call by their first names, but by what we have willingly done for each other. We may meet many people in the course of a short time and then not see them again for years, perhaps. We recognize their faces but do not know their hearts. That is not friendship but mere acquaintance, for there can be no real friendship where the heart is not involved or revealed.

—Beverly Coleman

It is fine to say "good morning;"
It is great to say "hello,"
But its better still to grasp the hands
Of the loyal friends you know;
For the look may be forgotten,
The words misunderstood,
But just the touch of a friendly hand
Is a pledge of brotherhood.

———

Do you think much of the friend who does not actually believe in you? He may not approve of all you do; he may be irritated at many of your actions; but if he has a real belief in your sincerity, he's your best friend. Many a person has gained a new meaning of life simply through putting his faith in another. If someone places his faith in us we should do all we can to justify that confidence.

One of the high offices of a friend is to rebuke us. That does not mean to be always finding fault and giving moral lessons about what we have not done. That would only disrupt friendship. The friends to whom we should show the greatest gratitude are those who have helped us to be our best, whose very qualities and standards have been a rebuke to us when we have become lax. The teachers for whom we have the most gratitude are those who reprimanded our laziness and indifference.

To say that a true friend lays an obligation on his friend is a strange thing, yet it is true that the expectations others have of us play a large part in our development.

As we think of these qualities of friendship we should ask ourselves whether our friendship with others carries any of these qualities, or if it has any of these effects on our friends.

—*Betty Hallowell*

———

Friendship is not confined to any particular geographical locality. No surveyed chart, no natural boundary line, no rugged mountain or deep vale puts a limit to its growth. Wherever it is watered with the dews of kindness and affection, there you may be sure to find it. Its influence dispels every poisonous thought of envy and spreads abroad in the heart a contentment which all the powers of the mind could not otherwise bestow.

Friendship blooms only in the soil of the noble and self-sacrificing heart; there it enjoys perpetual summer, diffusing a sweet atmosphere of love, peace and joy to all around.

No one can go very far, no matter what his strength and courage, if he goes alone through the weary struggles of life. We are made happier and better by each other's notice and appreciation and the hearts that are debarred from those influences invariably contract and harden.

Here and there we may find persons who from pride or singularity of disposition appear to be altogether indifferent to the notice or regard of their fellow-beings, but never yet was there a human heart that did not, at some time, long for the sympathy of others.

Friendship is like a garden of flowers rich and rare
It cannot reach perfection except through loving care.
Then new and lovely blossoms with each new day appear,
For friendship, like a garden, grows in beauty year by year.

True friendship has a sweetness that flavors all the years,
It banishes our worries and dries our springing tears,
It sets the heart to singing and starts the lips to smile.
Sometimes it seems that friendship is what makes life worth while.

There's a tribute that I want to pay
    To special friends like you,
And the folks that it would fit, I'll say,
    Are mighty, mighty few.
So I want, with all my heart and soul,
    To always prove to be
Your friend in need, your friend indeed,
    Just as you've been to me.

———

There are millions of folks in the world, it is true;
Millions of people—but only one you.
So I count myself lucky, and shall to the end,
That out of the millions I've you for a friend.

———

These are the things I prize
    And hold of dearest worth:
Light of the sapphire skies,
    Shadows of clouds that quickly pass,
The smell of flowers
    And of the good brown earth;
And, best of all, along the way
    Friendship and mirth.

———

We need our friends, but when all other friends fail us we
are never alone for our Eternal Friend walks beside us always.
He walks with us from the beginning of that ever begun but
never ending today. Can we merit the presence of such a

Friend unless we are true to our earthly friends? It has been well said, "A friend is one who knows all about you and still loves you." How many such friends do we have? A true friend wants to help us when we go wrong and stands by us when we are right. Many friendships have been broken by gossip or the wrong kind of politics. Let us try to avoid such heartaches. Let us not judge each other hastily or blindly. I wonder what the result would be if we approached our real enemies as we do our true friends—with a telescope rather than with a microscope. Let's try it.

—*Nancy Rickard*

No road of life runs smooth and straight.
There are many little lanes
That mark a change decreed by fate
For losses or for gains.
No road of life runs to the end
Without a hill or two;
But I won't mind the hills, my friend,
If I may climb with you.

Of all the blessings heaven doth send,
Of all the gifts that life doth lend,
Here's to the one who'll not pretend
But is, and stays, my steadfast friend.

We meet tonight on common ground
Old friendships to renew,
While hearts grow glad, and hand meets hand
In greetings warm and true.

Friendship

There are no friends like the old friends
Who shared our morning days,
No greeting like their welcome,
No homage like their praise.

Thine own friend, and thy father's friend, forsake not.
—*Proverbs 27:10*

Friendship in business means a lot. As a truly active force in the consummation of everyday business, none can deny its potency. Friendship can be cultivated through correspondence but it lacks that fine, personal touch which marks the final expression of real loyalty. The merchants of this community are your friends. Their interests are vital to your interests. They go to the same church you do; their children go to the same school as your children. They drive their cars over the same roads you use. Their interests are your interests—your interests are theirs. They are anxious to see you succeed in your undertakings; they want you to be prosperous and they will do everything in their power to help you. As you prosper, they prosper, the community prospers and everyone is happier, since a prosperous community is the best place in which to live.

The secret of friendship is just the secret of all spiritual blessing. The way to get is to give. The selfish, in the end, can never get anything but selfishness. The hard find hardness everywhere. As you give, it is given back to you.

Some men have a genius for friendship. That is because they are open and responsive and unselfish. They truly make the most of life; for apart from their special joys, even intellect is sharpened by the development of the affections. No material success in life is comparable to success in friendship. We really do ourselves harm by our selfish standards.

There is an old Latin proverb that says it is not possible for a man to love and at the same time to be wise. This is the worldly view and is only true when wisdom is made equal to prudence and selfishness, and when love is made the same. Rather, it is never given to a man to be wise in the true and noble sense until he has been carried out of himself in the purifying passion of love or the generosity of friendship. The self-centered being cannot keep friends, even when he makes them; his selfish sensitiveness is always in the way, like a diseased nerve, ready to be irritated.

———

We are richer because you have bestowed your friendship upon us. You have been an inspiration to each of us. You have taught us to be neighborly and how to make stepping stones out of stumbling blocks. We have watched you trace the handiwork of God in commonplace things of life, and to count out the things that really do not count. You have looked for the best in others and have given others the best in you, and in doing this you have made a host of loyal friends and neighbors.

—*Katie Hardt*

———

Friends, like jewels, grow dearer with years;
We value their worth beyond measure.
Time but strengthens and tightens each link
In friendship's gold chain that we treasure.

Sorrows grow lighter when clasping their hands,
Their comforting words give us healing,
Joys grow brighter, more blesséd, because
Their presence bespeaks a warm feeling.

———

It has been my joy this year to find,
At every turning of the road,
The strong arm of a comrade kind
To help me onward with my load.
And, since I have no gold to give
And love alone must make amends,
My only prayer is, while I live,
God, make me worthy of my friends.

———

The sweetness of remembrance,
    The love that friendship lends,
Combine to fill the heart with song
    In praise of loyal friends.
God bless the kindly spirit
    Which prompts each loving thought,
For with the gold of friendship
    Great riches you have brought.

The sweetness of remembrance
    Puts blue into the sky;
It drives away the shadows
    And makes the clouds roll by.
The little act of giving
    A kindly thought or two—
It makes your life worth living
    To know your friends are true.

                        —*Ella E. Van Court*

———

There are no friends like old friends,
And none so good and true.
We meet them and we greet them
As roses greet the dew.

No other friends are dearer,
Though born of kindred mould;
And while we prize the new friends
We treasure more the old.

———

There is a greater need today in our fraternal organizations for true friendship than perhaps at any other time in our history. Things seem so chaotic, people so careless, irresponsible and self-centered. We are drifting away from the church and from the old-fashioned yet ever-needed American home.

And yet—are we doing all in our power to help cope with these strange but existing conditions? Are people losing faith in us because we fail to live up to the standard of true friendship? Are we true to our own convictions of duty and right or are we just seeking popularity by walking with the crowd? When each of us entered our beautiful Order a friend in whom we trusted walked beside us. Is that same friend, with other Chapter members, still walking beside us in true friendship—the friendship each and every member pledges to cherish? Remember, "he who has a thousand friends has not a friend to spare; and he who has one enemy will meet him everywhere."

———

Good friends walked beside us
On the trails we tried to keep;
Our burden seemed less heavy
And the hills were not so steep.
The weary miles passed swiftly,
Taken in joyous stride,
And all the world was brighter
Because they walked by our side.

————

XIV

LOVE AND SERVICE

Love is an actual need, an urgent requirement of the heart,
and every properly constituted human being who entertains
an appreciation of loneliness and wretchedness and looks forward to happiness and contentment feels a necessity for love.
The love that is grander than any other, which is as powerful
today as in the morning of time, love that has the power to
tame the savage heart, which finds a man rough and unculti-
vated and selfish and leaves him a refined and courteous gentle-
man, which transforms the timid, bashful youth into a man of
matchless power for good, is the love of our heavenly Father
for us.

Of love we make life's guiding star
To shine along our daily ways;
Whatever we may say or do
Love is a constant theme of praise.

A year of planting deed on deed,
A year of sowing love's rare seed;
From out this radiant, starlit field
Let come a full love harvest-yield.
            —*Josie Frazee Cappleman*

Love—like soap, or pills or mustard—depends largely upon advertisement for its success.

—*Ellen Thornycroft Fowler*

———

In the Order of the Eastern Star we have an organization that is founded on the principles of love and service. We follow the principles of Him Whose manger birthplace was lighted with the Star of Bethlehem and Whose life of love and service transcends even that brightness.

We are proud of our place and opportunity of rendering love and service; we are proud of our friends, old and new, we are glad of the opportunity of being friends to others.

———

If you want to be happy
Then start right away
Doing one kindness
For someone each day.
Scatter some sunshine,
Forget about self,
And put all your worries
Away on a shelf.

If you want to be happy
Just begin to be glad;
Keep thinking of others
And never be sad;
Don't wait 'til tomorrow
But start right away
Just doing one kindness
For someone each day.

—*Marie Woerheide*

———

But once I pass this way,
  And then—no more.
But once—and then the silent door
Swings on its hinges—
Opens—closes—
  And no more
I pass this way.
So, while I may,
With all my might I will essay
Sweet comfort and delight
To all I meet upon the Pilgrim way.
For no man travels twice
  The Great Highway
That climbs through darkness up to light,
Through night
  To day.

—*John Oxenham*

———

To love someone more dearly every day,
To help a wandering child to find its way,
To ponder o'er a noble thought and pray,
And smile when evening comes,
This is my task.

———

"T—N—T"—Today, Not Tomorrow

———

The star in the heaven's blue was a service star hung by our Father over the hills of Judea many years ago. This Star to the shepherds meant amazement—to the Wise Men, a King —to us, service, and a message for our beautiful Order. In the star of our flag still shines the steadfastness of that star in the heaven, and it still lights the paths of men to courage, devotion and service.

———

Teach us, Good Lord, to serve Thee as Thou deserveth.
To give, and not to count the cost,
To fight and not to heed the wounds,
To toil and not to seek for rest,
To labor and not ask for any reward,
Save that of knowing that we do Thy will.
                              —*St. Ignatius Loyola*

———

I have lighted a candle of Service,
That we who have seen the Star
May think of our Sisters and Brothers
And help them wherever they are.
May envy and hate and malice
Wither before the flame,
And the eternal fires of God light up
Our hearts in the Father's name.

———

Shall service be for duty's sake alone—
A half unwilling help we merely give
To salve a conscience not yet callous grown,
Or to justify some right to live?

No service this; the eager, willing hand
Must be inspired to do its ordered part
By thoughtful mind where sturdy faith has planned,
Must be directed by the loving heart.

Who profits most by service? He who strives,
Who every moment of the day conserves
To bring some benefit to others' lives.
Who profits most by service? He who serves.

If we may offer up one special plea
To Him from whom our trust shall never swerve,
May this our constant prayer forever be,
Lord, give us *opportunity* to serve.
                    —*Frank W. Lynn*

———

A good action is never lost; it is a treasure laid up and
guarded for the doer's need.

———

No one is useless in the world who lightens the burden of
it for someone else.
                    —*Dickens*

———

There are loyal hearts, there are spirits brave,
There are those that are good and true,
So give to the world all the best that you have;
And the best will come back to you.

Give love, and love to your heart shall flow
A strength in your inmost need;
Have faith, and a score of hearts shall show
Their faith in your word and deed.

Give truth, and your gift will be paid in kind,
And honor will honor meet,
And a smile that is sweet will surely find
A smile that is just as sweet.

For life is the mirror of king and slave,
'Tis just what we are and do,
So give to the world all the best that you have,
And the best will come back to you.

THE UNSEEN GUEST

Since that far distant day
When He who had not where to lay His head
Within the house at Bethany was sheltered,
    warmed and fed,
A holier thing has come to be—
Our Christian hospitality:
For surely, when we pilgrim folk
Our tents with one another share,
And break our daily traveler's bread—
The Unseen Guest is there;
And you who give and we who take—
Twice blesséd are for His dear sake.

        —Hugh L. Burleson

I would rather have a rose bud from the garden of a friend
than to have my casket covered when my stay on earth shall
end. Let's strive to do more kind things while people live; they
do not need us when they are gone.

Lighthouses don't ring bells and fire cannon to call attention
to their shining; they just shine on.

A Vision without a Task is a Dream;
A Task without a Vision is Drudgery;
A Vision and a Task are the Hope of the World.

———

We all of us have a road to take—
That road is the road of Life.
Each of us has a share of joy
And each has a share of strife.
And since we all must travel that road
In sunny or stormy weather,
We each can lighten the other's load
If we all pull along together.

———

He has not served who gathers gold,
Nor has he served whose life is told
In selfish battles he has won
Or deeds of skill that he has done;
But he has served who now and then
Has helped along his fellow-men.

———

Real joy comes not from ease or riches or from the praise
of men, but from doing something worthwhile.
                                        —*Sir W. Grenfell*

———

Life is mostly froth and bubble;
    Two things stand like stone—
Kindness in another's trouble,
    Courage in our own.

———

Today is your day, and mine, the only day that we have, the day in which we play our part. What our part may signify in the great whole we may not understand, but we are here to play it, and now is our time. This we know: It is a part of action, not of whining. It is a part of love, not cynicism. It is for us to express love in terms of human helpfulness. This we know, for we have learned from sad experience that any other course of life leads toward decay and waste.

—David Starr Jordan

Never forget the little deeds of kindness and the little acts of love that make life one grand sweet song in which no Miserere is ever blended.

Let us give the bread, and never cast the stone; let us be generous in affection, forgiving in spirit, grateful for friendships unbroken, ever mindful of the burdens of others—for these are the principles of the Order of the Eastern Star, and this coinage in the currency of the universe shall remain when all else has become unhonored and forgotten.

There is something that lacks finality in the spoken word, while in the doing of an act of kindness there is an enduring result that is not only beneficial but constructive.

—T. V. Moreau

Did you ever know of a monument erected to preserve the memory of an evil deed? There may be some that have been erected to the memory of men who were powerful and abused their power, but these are few and rare compared to those erected to preserve the memory of deeds and men who have been both great and good. The tallest monument ever erected to a single man is the Washington monument and it is a monument not only to the man but to "Service." The broadest monument ever erected to a single man is the Lincoln monument and it also is a monument not only to the man, but to "Service."

The broken column should be to us, not only a reminder of the uncertainty of human life, but also a reminder that monuments are built to commemorate faithful service.

—*James A. Gibson*

The cause of human progress is our cause, the enfranchisement of human thought our supreme wish, the freedom of human conscience our mission, and the guarantee of equal rights to all peoples everywhere the end of our contention.

In our pursuit of the distant visionary things that we think will satisfy, we too often neglect the real opportunity that is knocking at our door.

In the present day of rush and drive there is serious danger of giving way to the temptation that we have not time to devote to the little duties of being thoughtful and kind. Not everyone who needs a cup of cold water is calling out to the world. The little pauses we make by the way are not wasted time. A word of sympathy, some little act that shows a friendly interest, may help the next hour to move more lightly and swiftly. And it is one of the most beautiful compensations in this life that no man can sincerely try to help another without helping himself.

THINGS WORTH WHILE

Don't ask, "Has the world been a friend to me?"
But "Have I to the world been true?"
'Tis not what you get but what you give
That makes life worth while to you.
'Tis the kind word said to the little child
As you wiped its tears away
And the smile you brought to some careworn. face
That really lights up your day.

'Tis the hand you clasp with an honest grasp
That gives you a hearty thrill.
'Tis the good you pour into other lives
That comes back your own to fill.
'Tis the dregs you drain from another's cup
That makes your own seem sweet,
And the hours you give to your fellow-men
That make your own life complete.

'Tis the burdens you help another bear
That make your own seem light.
'Tis the danger seen for another's feet
That shows you the path to right.
'Tis the good you do each passing day
With a heart that's sincere and true,
For through giving the world your very best
Its best will return to you.

—Mabel Brown Denison

IS ANYBODY HAPPIER?

Is anybody happier because you passed his way?
Does anyone remember that you spoke to him today?
This day is almost over and its toiling time is through;
Is there anyone to utter now a kindly word of you?

Did you give a cheerful greeting to the friend who
  came along?
Or a churlish sort of "howdy" and then vanish in the
  throng?
Were you selfish, pure and simple, as you rushed
  along your way?
Or is someone mighty grateful for a deed you did today?

Can you say tonight, in parting with the day that's
  slipping fast,
That you helped a single brother of the many that you
  passed?
Is a single heart rejoicing over what you did or said?
Does a man whose hopes were fading now with courage
  look ahead?

Did you waste the day or use it; was it well or poorly
  spent?
Did you leave a trail of kindness or a scar of discontent?
As you close your eyes in slumber do you think that
  God would say
You have earned one more tomorrow by the work you
  did today?

———

It isn't buildings of steel and stone
   That the world needs most today,
It isn't fame and it isn't gold,
   It isn't the knowledge that textbooks hold—
That is the smaller part.
It's the kindlier smile and friendlier hand,
   The love that knows no creed nor land,
But speaks from heart to heart.

———

A thousand roadways lead to Rome,
   But love has only one—
The little trail that hurries home
   Beneath the setting sun.

A thousand stars light up the skies,
   Love has a single flame—
The glow that kindles in the eyes
   At mention of a name.

A thousand flowers fill the earth,
   Love has one petal scent—
The tiny rose whose magic birth
   Gives us God's sacrament.

———

We must share, if we would keep
Those blessings from above.
Ceasing to give, we cease to have.
Such is the law of Love.

———

Days of planning, days of pleasure,
So our year has come and gone;
As your works, so your reward is,
Loving acts live on and on!

———

So let us at all times exemplify the true meaning of fraternity by putting our souls into every hand clasp, greet each other with a smile and enjoy life's sunshine together, for they who sow courtesy reap friendship and they who plant kindness gather love.

———

Lose yourself in some opportunity to bring cheer to the world—and you will instantly experience a joy that is more desirable than pursuit of selfish ends.

———

To love the Lord, with all thy heart
　　And all thy strength and mind
To do a friendly neighbor's part,
　　To every one be kind.
This is the law, the Master gave,
　　As comprehending all
Our duty, this side of the grave
　　Until ye hear His call.

Then let us one another love,
　　As through this life we go,
And lay up for ourselves above,
　　While we live here below,
Rich treasures which will never fade,
　　Eternal bright and fair,
When mortal bodies here are laid
　　Our spirits over there.
　　　　　　　　—Jesse Edmondston

———

XV

GOOD OF THE ORDER

SISTERS AND BROTHERS, give thought to the great heritage that has come to you from the founders of this Order. Help to reflect their beauty by your beneficence; their purpose to make the world better by better living yourselves; make their high and holy teachings the rule and guide for your conduct. Be steadfast in your fidelity, constant in your humility, loyal to your trusts, unswerving in your faith, and, above all, follow the lesson commanded by the Master and taught by Electa—"love one another." Some one has said, "If you believe in God, live so that others will believe in Him." If you believe in the principles of our Order, live so others will also believe.

———

What every member should do: Learn thoroughly the things for which the Order stands.

Read the laws by which your Chapter is governed.

Attend your Chapter meetings.

Participate in the deliberations of the Chapter.

Get better acquainted with the officers and members of your Chapter.

If you will do these things you will make your Chapter better and profit more from your membership. There is no room for lax officers in a Chapter of live-wire members. Take your stand in the front line; understand the responsibilities of the officers; work for all, that you may share in the making of a Chapter of which all its members may be proud.

———

After this meeting closes and we have gone home and had a little time to reflect and meditate over what has taken place this evening, may we resolve to live within the teachings of this great Organization and within the boundaries of our grand Obligation, for by so doing we will be better citizens, better neighbors, better mothers and fathers and, last but not least, better Eastern Star members.

———

To every sincere member of the Order the ballot box should hold a deep significance. In our privilege of accepting or rejecting the petitions for membership that come to us is involved all the responsibility of our vows at the altar. Stop before you cast your ballot; listen closely to that unerring inner voice that speaks calmly and surely in each of us; be guided by that clear, unchanging ray of light that shines always across the depth of the heart. Vote, not lightly, not carelessly, not moved by the petty opinions of superficial life, but cast the good ballot—the ballot you know is fair and right.

———

In entering the Eastern Star we enter upon a new phase of life and should get away from the idea that we merely "belong" to the Order but should go forth into the world to live what we have been taught: Love one another; teach one another; help one another. That is our doctrine, our science, our law, and we endeavor to improve our social order by enlightening our minds and warming our hearts by the good and discarding the bad in all things.

———

We should ever be mindful at all times and under all conditions that the Star of Bethlehem is, and should be, our inspiration. It should guide our footsteps and make our pathway glow as we follow in the steps of the Master.

———

We are building a wonderful structure for all to see, a structure whose foundation is laid on sterling qualities and the highest ideals. This structure is supported by the great union of our purpose and devotion to the best interest of all. Its walls are made of wonderful loyalty to our convictions of right and duty, as outlined in our teachings, and around and about and over all is the greatest of all lessons—charity and love, for our fellow beings.

I belong to the Order of the Eastern Star and know that its teachings are the very pillars of aesthetics and morals, the very music of God's religion, and therefore would pass on to you His word. For I know that in an age and day like this, when the foundations of society are trembling, when it has been said that another twenty-five years will tell whether this world will be Christian or communistic, I know that you and I can transform society if we will "live the poetry we sing," if we will live up to the sublime and beautiful principles of this great and Christian Order.

The Order of the Eastern Star exists for no selfish purpose. It means more to us than our association in the Chapter, more than the technical business of each administration, fine as they are. Our Order is built upon principle and inculcates the lesson of duty. We are concerned with the things that make character, that ennoble individual lives and through them the community in which we live. As we look out upon the horizon of the future and dimly see the responsibilities and duties that lie before us, may the Star of Bethlehem, that beautiful symbol of our Order, guide us and inspire us with an ambition to acquire those sublime virtues exemplified by the heroines of our Order, and strengthen our hearts for the great work we strive to do. —*Matilda E. Kinne.*

Throw away your wishbone; stiffen your backbone; stick out your jawbone; go out and win.

———

Drop a pebble in the water
And its ripples reach out far,
And the sunbeams dancing on them
May reflect them to a star.

Give a smile to someone passing,
Thereby make their morning glad;
It may meet you in the evening
When your own heart may be sad.

Do a deed of simple kindness.
Though its end you may not see,
It may reach, like widening ripples,
Down a long eternity.

———

We live in a challenging age. How good it is to be alive today. What strength of character it gives us to face a problem squarely and with open minds attempt its solution. We do not, and cannot, always succeed, but the measure of greatness is not to be tested by achievement but by the effort made and the knowledge that success will come if we are faithful and do not grow weary. We who have seen His Star in the East have cause for rejoicing. It is true we are not as numerically strong as we once were; our bank accounts are not as large; but we are, as never before, a united, happy family—all for one and one for all. We have learned the great lesson of giving—not of our excess, but of our very own, sharing with others our joys and comforting those in sorrow.

———

What is the Order of the Eastern Star? A meeting ground
For those of purpose great and broad and strong,
Whose aim is in the stars, who ever long
To make the patient, listening earth resound
With sweeter music, purer, freer tones;
A place where kindly lifting words are said,
Where kindlier deeds are done—where hearts are fed;
Where wealth of brain for poverty atones,
Where hand grasps hand and soul finds touch with soul,
Where victors in the race for fame and power
Look backward, even in their triumph hour,
To beckon others to the shining goal.
All this is what the Eastern Star should be, a haven fair,
Where we may drop, for a brief hour, our load of care.

———

XVI

MISCELLANEOUS

MAY joy and comfort greatly bless
And fill your days with happiness,
And may your heart be filled with cheer,
And sweet contentment through the year.

———

Our Star is the book,
The members are the leaves,
The officers are the cover
That protective beauty gives.

At first the pages of the book
Are blank and purely fair,
But time soon writeth memories
And painteth pictures there.

Love is the golden clasp
That bindeth up the trust.
O, break it not, lest all the leaves
Shall scatter and be lost.

———

A PRAYER

Supreme Ruler of the Universe:
Open my eyes that I may see the truth;
Open my mind that I may receive the truth,
Inspire my soul that I may live the truth,
Lest I die, having never lived.

—*James W. Smith*

———

Trials, temptations, disappointments, all these are helps instead of hindrances, if one uses them rightly. They not only test the fiber of character, but strengthen it. Every conquered temptation represents a new fund of moral energy. Every trial endured, if weathered in the right spirit, makes a soul nobler and stronger than it was before.

—*James Buckham*

———

Happiness consists not in possessing enough, but in being content with what we possess. He who wants little always has enough.

———

The days grow shorter, the nights grow longer,
The headstones thicker along the way;
And life grows sadder, but love grows stronger
For those who walk with us day by day.
Then let us clasp hands as we walk together,
And let us speak softly, in love's sweet tone,
For no man knows on the morrow whether
We two pass by, or one alone.

———

You can constantly find in others something good to praise and endorse. The habit of generous appreciation of others not only exalts you mentally but profoundly affects their lives also. If you would make men praiseworthy, praise them.

Years of happy labor
Have builded a temple fair;
Love was its inspiration,
And Faith laid the cornerstone there.

THE GREAT CLOCK

The clock of life is wound but once,
 And no man has the power
To tell just when the hand will stop—
 At late or early hour.
Now is the only time you own;
 Live, love, toil with a will;
Place no faith in to-morrow, for
 The clock may then be still.

Life is a grindstone, and whether it grinds us down or polishes us up depends on the stuff of which we are made.

This evening we are honored with the
 officers of yore;
They will man the Chapter from
 the East to outer door.
They are the dear old "has-beens"
 who helped us see the Star—
Honored for what they have been;
 loved for what they are.

THE MATRON'S HUSBAND

I am the goat of this whole affair.
I have to run errands to goodness knows where.
Hear Eastern Star talk three times a day,
Eat cold meals, or none, or any old way;
And through it all I must keep sweet as I can.
I am not my own self—just the Matron's old man
—Eastern Star Review—Toronto

———

A bird at your window to sing you a song,
A rose in your garden to bloom the day long,
A rainbow of hope that brings comfort and cheer,
A star in the sky when shadows appear,
The smile of a friend who is loyal and true—
May these be the joys each day holds for you.

———

There's a star in the east and it shineth today
On the dear lands of home and the lands far away,
It shineth abroad over mountain and sea,
It shineth, my Sister, for you and for me.

It shone long ago, first in Bethlehem town
On that clear silent night that the Savior came down
Bringing peace and good will from the Father above.
'Twas the symbol He gave of His wonderful love.

It lighted the hillside where angels did sing.
Shone on Wise Men who came bearing gifts for the King;
On the meek and the lowly, the mighty and great,
From the low stable door to the wide palace gate.

It comforted hearts that were weary and sad;
   Sin-burdened souls were made happy and glad.
It lighted the darkness of evil, and then
   Gave courage and hope to the children of men.

There's a star in the East and it shineth today
   On the dear lands of home and the lands far away.
It shineth abroad over mountain and sea,
   It shineth, my Sister, for you and for me.

―――――

A rose, half-blown, may be regarded as a symbol of human life, which, however beautiful, may always grow into greater perfection.

―――――

In memory's sunny garden down pleasant paths I'll stray
All along with happy thoughts of you and yesterday.
Our golden hours together, their happiness renew,
And all my thoughts will be sweet dreams of yesterday and you.

―――――

What prompts the farmer to earnest toil,
To plow, and cultivate the soil?
'Tis faith that sunshine, clouds and rain
Will crown his work with fruitful gain.

Why does the Architect display
His skill, and labor day by day?
In order that before his eyes
A great skyscraper may arise.

'Tis faith in what he has at heart
That nerves him from the very start,
That keeps him working every day
And makes his labor seem like play.

Thus faith is proven by the deeds
Which men perform. It always leads
Them on to greater brighter things;
And with applause the whole world rings.

And so it is with us as we
Our journeys take by land or sea,
For by our work our faith is shown,
And by our labor we are known.

If we have faith in what we say,
Believe in all we do each day,
Our labor will proclaim aloud
That we are by true faith endowed.

—*Jesse Edmonston*

We cannot all do great things, but we can all do small things in a great way. Always remember—

A man's no bigger than the way
    He treats his fellow man.
This standard has his measure been
    Since time itself began.
He's measured not by tithes or creed,
    High-sounding though they be,
Nor by the gold that's put aside,
    Nor by his sanctity.

He's measured not by social rank
  When character's the test;
Nor by his earthly pomp or show,
  Displaying wealth possessed.
He's measured by his justice, right,
  His fairness at his play,
His squareness in all dealing made,
  His honest, upright way.
These are his measures, ever near
  To serve him when they can;
For man's no bigger than the way
  He treats his fellow man.

———

All higher motives, ideals, conceptions, sentiments in a man are of no account if they do not come forward to strengthen him for the better discharge of the duties which devolve upon him in the ordinary affairs of life.

—*Henry Ward Beecher*

———

In the Garden of Fraternity,
The soft winds gently blow—
To fan the sparks of kindness
That you and I may show!

———

We are passing through a strenuous period; everyone has his share of worries; everyone is rushing in an effort to make both ends meet; yet we can still find time to be charitable and loving and not forget to do the little kindly acts that go to make life happier. It costs nothing to give a smile—unless perchance it hides a little heartache—yet that consideration is small compared to the value of a genuine, friendly smile; therefore, may we choose a smile for our daily decoration and, at least, help to brighten a more or less somber picture.

THE VALUE OF A SMILE

It costs nothing, but creates much.

It enriches those who receive without impoverishing those who give.

It happens in a flash and the memory of it sometimes lasts forever.

None is so rich he can get along without it, nor so poor but is richer for its benefits.

It creates happiness in the home, fosters good will in a business, and is the countersign of friends.

It is rest to the weary, daylight to the discouraged, sunshine to the sad, and Nature's best antidote for trouble.

Yet it cannot be bought, begged, borrowed, or stolen, for it is something that is no earthly good to anybody till it is given away.

Nobody needs a smile so much as he who has none left to give.

FACE THE SUN

Don't grumble, don't bluster, don't dream, and don't shirk;
Don't think of your worries, but think of your work.
The worries will vanish, the work will be done,
For none sees his shadow while facing the sun.

It only takes a little love to make this life more sweet,
It only takes a little cheer to make the day complete,
It only takes a little smile to brighten all the day,
So plan a little bit of each for all who come your way.

———

There is a destiny that makes us brothers:
  None goes his way alone.
All that we send into the lives of others
  Comes back into our own.

—*Edwin Markham*

———

We are building every day
In a good or evil way,
And the structure, as it grows,
Will our inmost self disclose
Till in every arch and line
All our faults and virtues shine.
It may grow a castle grand,
Or a wreck upon the sand.

Do you ask what building this
That can show both pain and bliss,
That can be both dark and fair?
Lo! its name is Character!
Build it well, whate'er you do;
Build it straight and strong and true,
Build it clean and high and broad,
Build it for the eyes of God.

———

LIVING BOUQUETS

When I shall quit this mortal shore
And mosey round this earth no more,
Please do not mourn, nor sigh, nor sob;
I may have struck a better job.

Don't go and buy a large bouquet
For which you find it hard to pay;
Don't mope around and feel all blue;
I may be better off than you.

If you have roses,—bless your soul,
Just pin one in my buttonhole
While I'm alive and well today;
Don't wait until I've gone away.

Don't tell the folks I was a saint
Or any old thing which I ain't;
If you have jam like that to spread
Please hand it out before I'm dead.

—Cora Posey

———

Oh, it's great to be a matron,
   And with the matrons stand;
A patron at your left side,
   A gavel in your hand.
And though we have our ups and downs,
   Right merry still we'll be,
For we are matrons just for "now"—
   Not for eternity.

———

CLOSING ODE

Air: Taps

Fading light
Dims the sight,
And a Star
Gems the sky,
Gleaming bright
From afar.
Drawing nigh
Falls the night.
So our day
Nears its end,
As we stand,
Touching hands
'Neath the glow
Of our Star.
O. E. S.
Says good night.

———

God bless you now and evermore
Your days with gladness crown;
And from His own abundant store
Send many a blessing down.

———

Memory's lane is a clear little path
Where hearts are ever true,
A path I will travel again and again
Because it leads to you.

———

There are folks with whom you feel at home
And folks with whom you don't;
There are folks with whom you'll have good times,
And folks with whom you won't.
But young folks, old folks, good and true folks,
Search the wide world through;
No other folks on all this earth
Are half so nice as you.

———

Bless this Chapter and all within it,
Let no harsh spirit enter in it.
Let none approach who would betray;
None with a bitter word to say.
Grant that these friends from year to year
May build their happiest memories here.

Bless this Chapter and those who love it,
Fair be the skies which bend above it,
Endow this place with lasting wealth—
The light of love, the glow of health.
In the sweet oils of gladness steep it
God bless this Chapter and those who keep it.

———

This good old world would be better
If the folks we meet would say;
"I know something good about you."
And treat us just that way.
It would be fine and dandy
If each hand clasp warm and true
Carried with it that message
"I know something good about you."

———

There's a Star, such a wonderful Star,
That is guiding us on through life's way,
And its beautiful rays, near and far,
Give us courage and hope day by day.

With the blue of the sky it is dowered,
And the gold of the well-ripened grain,
With the white of a pure lily flowered
That a lesson we mortals may gain.

With the green, that the Father above
May be given His true meed of praise,
And the red, glowing symbol of love,
To make brighter the darkest of days.

————

THE FINAL VERDICT

Ere long we'll face life's evening,
   And view with pride or shame
The record of our journey—
   The maze through which we came;
And he who keeps the records
   No soul has ever wronged;
He'll write, "In truth an Eastern Star"
   Or that "She just belonged."

————

It is not only natural for man to believe in something—it
is absolutely essential.

————

Kindly, generous thought from each of us is the first step
toward a righteous world.

————

So many stars in the infinite space—
So many worlds in the light of God's face.

So many storms ere the thunders shall cease—
So many paths to the portals of peace.

So many years, so many tears—
Sighs and sorrows and pangs and prayers.

So many ships in the desolate night—
So many harbors, and only one Light.

So many creeds like the weeds in the sod—
So many temples, but only one God.

—*Frank L. Stanton*

So many gods, so many creeds,
So many ways that wind and wind,
While just the art of being kind
Is all this old world needs.

—*Ella Wheeler Wilcox*

We live in the present; we dream of the future; and we learn eternal truths from the past.

—*Mme. Chiang Kai-shek*

May God dwell in the garden of our Star.

The Eastern Star Flag:

It has been said that "Flags are born of high hopes and treasured memories" and when we behold our Eastern Star flag we can join in saying:

God bless this flag that we in reverence hold;
Shine on, O Star, may your lessons ne'er grow old,
May your precepts be proclaimed both near and far.
Shine on, and we will follow, Oh, beautiful Eastern Star.

———

The bar that is blue bears a message to all:
Be loyal, be true in your acts, great or small.
The bar that is yellow denotes constancy—
Of all that is lovely a symbol shall be.
The white bar, whose fairness no blemish shall mar,
Sheds light and joy, helping us follow the Star.
Nature's own life eternal, portrayed by the green,
Speaks softly of faith and hope, calm and serene.
The bar that is red, and with fervency glows,
Bids us love one another, though cup overflows.
As thy gentle beams aid us in crossing the bar,
May we trustingly, faithfully, follow the Star.

—*Bertha Mauney*

———

XVII

PATRIOTIC SENTIMENTS

I pledge allegiance to the flag of the United States of America and to the Republic for which it stands, one Nation under God, indivisible, with liberty and justice for all.

———

I pledge allegiance to the Christian flag, and to the Savior for Whose kingdom it shines, one brotherhood uniting all mankind in service here.

———

I was born an American; I live an American; I shall die an American.

—*Daniel Webster*

———

We in the United States should count ourselves fortunate that we live under a Constitution which guarantees freedom of expression. Those who have never known anything but freedom can never appreciate its blessings to the full. Truth and liberty refuse to be suppressed. No matter how great the danger or severe the penalty, men will be found who treasure spiritual freedom above physical punishment. Even death does not deter them.

———

There can be no fifty-fifty Americanism in this country. There is room here only for those who are Americans and nothing else.

—*Theodore Roosevelt*

———

Guard, O God, our flag forever;
May dishonor stain it never;
To a grander future speed it;
In the paths of peace still lead it.

———

It remains a fact that the best salute to the flag in this land is good citizenship. No flag waving, no flowery oratory, no good writing, can take the place of it.

———

Liberty is not a gift; liberty has to be worked for continually; the responsibility never ceases. Only by our own labor and protection can we hold this privilege of freedom.

———

To the south there is a border line separating California from Mexico and the Central and South American Republics. To the north there is a border line between the United States and Canada. But we are one people, we of the American continents, and together we must, by our strength and might, keep liberty alive in the New World today, tomorrow, and for all time.

———

The union of lakes, the union of lands,
The union of states none can sever,
The union of hearts, the union of hands,
And the flag of our Union forever.

"Old Glory"
May your red remain a symbol of heavenly love that is sure;
May your white remain a token that from hatred we are pure;
May your blue and your stars ever point to the sky,
Our thoughts to turn Godward, our aims to make high!
Oh, beautiful banner, long may you wave
The flag of a people staunch, humble and brave.

—Abigail Cole

ABRAHAM LINCOLN

Abraham Lincoln! Speak the name with reverence. No greater-hearted man was ever born into this world than Lincoln.

With Washington, he stands a giant in the history of our nation. Yet he began life with no advantages of any kind. All that he gained, all that he made of his life, he wrested from it by the force of his will and the firmness of his purpose. Robert G. Ingersoll wrote: "It is the glory of Lincoln that, having almost absolute power, he never abused it, except on the side of mercy. Wealth could not purchase, power could not awe, this divine, this loving man. He knew no fear except the fear of doing wrong."

Calvin Coolidge said of Lincoln: "In wisdom great, but in humanity greater; in justice strong, but in compassion stronger; he became a leader of men by being a follower of truth."

O Beautiful, our country!
Round thee in love we draw;
Thine is the grace of freedom,
The majesty of law.
Be righteousness thy scepter,
Justice thy diadem,
And on thy shining forehead
Be peace the crowning gem!

———

America has furnished to the world the character of Washington. And if our American institutions had done nothing else, that alone would have entitled them to the respect of mankind

—*Daniel Webster*

God grants liberty only to those who love it and are always ready to guard and defend it.

—*Daniel Webster*

———

The man who kindles the fire on the hearthstone of an honest and righteous home burns the best incense to liberty. He does not love mankind less who loves his neighbor more. Exalt the citizen. As the State is the unit of government, he is the unit of the State. Teach him that his home is his castle and his sovereignty rests beneath his hat. Make him self-respecting, self-reliant and responsible. Let him lean on the State for nothing that his own arm can do, and on the Government for nothing that his State can do. Let him cultivate independence to the point of sacrifice and learn that humble things, with unbartered liberty, are better than splendors bought with a price.

—*Henry W. Grady*

———

Our Flag: The only bond that unites every American to every other regardless of race, creed or condition in life.

––––––

The symbol of a nation is its flag. It represents the living country and is itself considered a living thing. When we uphold and honor our country's flag we are supporting our country itself and all that it means to us.

There were several different flags in Colonial times but the first real American flag—our Stars and Stripes—had its origin in the following resolution adopted by the American Congress June 14, 1777: "Resolved: That the union be 13 stars, white on a blue field, representing a new Constellation."

On recommendation a committee composed of Washington, Robert Morris and Col. George Ross designed the flag and it was made by Col. Ross' wife, Betsy, who was an expert and professional needlewoman. Washington said of this flag: "We take the star from heaven, the red from our mother country, separating it by white stripes, thus showing that we have separated from her, and the white stripes shall go down to posterity representing liberty."

—Annie Schneider

––––––

Let us remember as we look at our flag, the symbol of our nation, that its red represents human sacrifices; its white, the shining purity of great lives which have been woven into it; and the stars, the hope in the hearts of all for a greater, nobler, holier America. The Star and Stripes are our crystallized hopes and fears—the symbol of our nation's glory. Those who made it, lived for it and died for it and are our nation's heroes. They have passed into the silence of history but by their devotion and courage and the splendor of their lives they ask us to be the flag-makers of today, making its red a little deeper by our sacrifices, its white more gleaming by the purity of our lives, its blue more like the blue of heaven because of our loyalty, and its stars brighter by our devotion to their highest hopes.

So let us work and live that this flag will never fly over injustice, tyranny, and oppression, but ever and always over righteousness, over a people made happy by kindness, love and goodness.

—Annie Schneider

———

God give us men; the time demands
Strong minds, great hearts, true faith and willing hands;
Men whom the lust of office does not kill;
Men whom the spoils of office cannot buy;
Men who possess opinions and a will;
Men who have honor; men who will not lie;
Men who can stand before a demagogue
And damn his treacherous flatteries without shrinking;
Tall men, sun-crowned, who live above the fog
In public duty and in private thinking—
    God give us men!

—J. G. Holland

———

O, beautiful Flag! We love three, we adore thee, we honor thee; the sound of thy name, the very sight of thee, thrills the heart of every true American.

Thy red—symbolical of the blood shed by thy sons and daughters to keep thee afloat and save thee from disgrace.

Thy white—symbolizing the purity of purpose with which you have entered every combat, making it possible for God to bring you through victorious.

Thy blue—symbolical of the fidelity of thy people to the laws and constitution of the land over which you float.

O, beautiful Flag, we love thee! May the gleam of thy bars and the light of thy stars forever thrill the hearts of thy people.

North, South, East and West,
Rise and join your hands—
Native born and brothers drawn
From many fatherlands.
Rise, ye nation of the morn,
Land where liberty was born;
Ye who fear no ruler's nod—
Ye who only kneel to God—
Rise! Salute the flag!

As our Star leads us to the Star of Bethlehem, so the stars in our flag lead us to the sanctuary where liberty, light and happiness are enjoyed.

Whene'er I see the flag go by
It thrills me through and through;
I stand "attention" and salute
The red, the white, the blue.

God bless the land o'er which it waves,
Its men and women, too,
And may it always be their pride,
The red, the white, the blue.

Then, God of Nations, hear us now
While we our pledge renew—
Allegiance to that Flag of Flags,
The red, the white, the blue.

Our Flag!

> Here's to the red of it—
> There's not a thread of it,
> Nor a shred of it,
> In all the spread of it
>   From foot to head,
> But heroes have died for it,
> Faced steel and lead for it,
> Precious blood shed for it,
>   Bathing it red.
>
> Here's to the white of it—
> Thrilled by the sight of it,
> Who knows the right of it
> But feels the might of it,
>   Through day and night?
> Womanhood's care for it
> Made manhood dare for it;
> Purity's prayer for it
>   Keeps it so white.
>
> Here's to the blue of it—
> Heavenly view of it,
> Star-spangled hue of it,
> Honesty's due of it,
>   Constant and true.
> Here's to the whole of it—
> Stars, stripes and pole of it,—
> Here's to the soul of it—
>   Red, white and Blue.
>   —*John J. Daly*

"Let us have faith that right makes might, and in that faith let us, to the end, dare to do our duty as we understand it."

—*Abraham Lincoln*

Our Flag, with your folds of white and scarlet and your silvery stars. Fond eyes welcome you, warm hearts cherish you, and dying lips give you their blessing. Ours by inheritance, ours by allegiance, ours by affection. Emblem of liberty! Hope of the world! Long may you float on the free winds of heaven.

Flag of the United States of America—the Stars and Stripes! What does it mean today? The exact details of its origin may be unknown but the story of its accomplishments and virtues will live as long as the mind of man continues to function.

What is it? It is the emblem of true democracy. Its history in war is glorious. From the time of its first struggles for freedom down to the Second World War it paid no tribute, yielded no territory. The world today is torn with war. Nation is attacking nation; empire giving battle to empire; yet we, over whom that flag flies, are maintaining our balance and sanity, working steadily for universal peace although doing our part to crush forever those who would banish freedom and democracy from the world.

In the world crisis of today, in our hopes for peace, for right thinking, for justice between nations as between men, our flag is destined to continue as one of the dominant forces of the world. This must be. The standard on which it floats is so high that if it ever falls—which God forbid!—civilization itself is liable to fall with it.

Therefore, let us consecrate ourselves anew, as Americans,

to defend it in the conflict of war as in the tranquillity of peace, in the combined spirit of Americanism and Freemasonry, which stand for one and the same thing.

We salute the Banner of Peace—Old Glory!

———

Our beloved country is now actively engaged in war against nations who seek to ruthlessly eliminate from this world all the things that we hold dear, and without which life, for us, would not be worth living. This world-wide conflict has already had a vital effect upon each of us and as time passes there is no doubt but that its effect will increase many fold. There can be but one answer from every Eastern Star member, young and old, and that is to do our utmost at whatever sacrifice, both as individuals and as an organization, to the end that man's right to liberty, justice and the pursuit of happiness shall not perish from the earth.

———

I believe in the United States of America as a government of the people, by the people, for the people, whose just powers are derived from the consent of the governed; a democracy in a republic; a sovereign nation of many sovereign states; a perfect union, one and inseparable, established upon those principles of freedom, equality, justice and humanity for which American patriots sacrificed their lives and their private fortunes. I therefore believe it is my duty to my country to love it; to support its Constitution; to obey its laws; to respect its flag; and to defend it against all enemies.

—*William Tyler Page*

———

As an American I am confident that no living citizen, no matter how exalted his position, no matter how intelligent he may be, and no matter how fervent his patriotism, is competent to deliver an adequate tribute to Old Glory—to Americans the most beautiful of all flags and symbolic of the power, the glory, and the freedom of a great nation. The only proper tribute to our flag is the silent, yet eloquent, homage of those who heroically made the supreme sacrifice in its defense. Yet we, who are living, should and must, even though our attempts be woefully feeble, pay homage to our flag whenever the opportunity presents itself.

———

Today when chaos, greed and unrest permeate the whole world we should give thanks to God that we live under the protection of our glorious flag. Fraternal orders are being persecuted and suppressed in many countries of the world today; so let us be eternally grateful that we are privileged to meet together and carry on the activities of our Order with the freedom that is our heritage.

———

What a privilege is ours in these days of world chaos to be able to utter those magic words—I am an American. Never was there a time when there was such necessity to put one's best thought and emotions to work on the problems of defense and peace as now. One needs to use all the native ingenuity and training one can acquire to keep democracy safe and alive.

———

We are only commencing to realize the seriousness of the world's greatest problem of all, the problem of government and reconstruction when this great strife is over. We must realize more than ever before the great need of our support in the cause of national defense. We must stand back of our boys who are called into the service of our country. Let us determine to broaden the horizon of our daily lives. Life is an immense problem—live it to its fullest. Greet each day with the cheer that comes from a heart filled with courage and kindness. Meet each new experience, pleasant or trying, with the determination to give of our best. Each day of life is an opportunity, a test, a duty, and as we sow so shall we reap. In ourselves lies all power of life, hence the future depends upon our individual acts. Let us make the most of every opportunity. On this depends our reward. It is blessed to rejoice in the past but even more to plan for the future. Let us profit by our mistakes and look to the future with a heart full of courage and cheer.

———

Over one hundred and sixty years ago our forefathers fought for and won their liberty, independence and right to live as free men. It is our birthright—bitterly fought for and won—preserved and protected by their lifeblood. It is this birthright of freedom and liberty that is now so sinisterly threatened and which we must insure as a heritage for posterity.

The gauntlet has again been thrown down and we, a united people, have answered the challenge with the determination of freemen. Our internal differences have been forgotten in a common cause—the defense and preservation of the sacred principles upon which this great nation is founded. It is with this purpose that we have again taken up arms.

The Eastern Star symbolizes the strongest bond of a free people—fraternalism. Were we to dissociate the meaning of the word "fraternalism" from within the bounds of the Chapter room and apply its meaning literally to our every day lives, to all with whom we come in contact, we of the Eastern Star, as individuals, would be contributing more toward the building of a strong citizen morale to carry this country through the dark days ahead, than any other factor.

Let us think of this nation as one great fraternity through which we are all striving to preserve the birthright of our children and the children of generations to come. Let us forget petty grievances and work together, coordinating our efforts into one gigantic endeavor symbolic of true fraternalism. Let us, through the teachings of our Order, insure the perpetuation of the Great Fraternity of these United States that "this government of the people, by the people, for the people, shall not perish from the earth."

—*Marjorie Cain Childress.*

---

3 FLAG TRIBUTES
by Frances Tuggle Parker, Grand Marshal

TO THE U.S.A. FLAG

It is an established custom among subordinate chapters of the Order of the Eastern Star to set aside a few minutes occasionally as a mark of loyalty to our Country and a tribute to its Flag.

We are proud of our flag. Proud because of the history of accomplishment that has taken place beneath its folds, but our pride in that history is by right of inheritance only, as we had no part in its making. Sacrifice of life and fortune in the days of the American Revolution made possible the birth of this Nation, and the permanence of the Stars and Stripes, and we are the inheritors of the greatness of the patriots of that day, and the beneficiaries of their historic service.

We should work for the public good and for the best interests of the country as a whole, and in doing so, we are worthy of our Great Inheritance.

It is up to us as members of the Eastern Star to be found always battling for the right "as God gives us power to see the right" and in no better way, in no higher way, can we pay tribute to that flag.

We gaze on our flag with love and affection. We see there represented the red of the sacrificial blood of our defending heroes shed that we might enjoy a free land where all men are equal. The white typifying a purity of life and conduct so essential to all Americans. The blue, taken from the eternal dome of Heaven, symbolic of limitless opportunity for service to all mankind, and the Stars—like the Star in the East, lighting the way and guiding us in the straight pathway.

Your flag, my flag, all hail, the flag of the dear old United States, we salute thee!

TO THE CHRISTIAN FLAG

The Christian flag is the banner of the Prince of Peace, and is the only flag to which the National Ensign shows submission. It stands for no creed or denomination. It contains no symbol of warfare. The ground is white, representing peace and purity; the blue field, the color of the unclouded sky, the symbol of fidelity and truth. Its chief device, the cross of red, is the emblem of Christian sacrifice, and reminds us that upon the cross, Christ made the supreme sacrifice that we might have the assurance of immortal life.

TO THE EASTERN STAR FLAG

The Eastern Star flag is deeply enshrined in the heart of each one of us here. A flag, on whose field, a five-pointed Star is enthroned. Each point, symbolic of a beautiful character, each character teaching a lesson of faith and loyalty, honor and justice, truth and sublime courage, and above all is LOVE.

So, with my hand on my heart, I salute you, beautiful flag of the Order of the Eastern Star. May all who find shelter beneath your folds, find peace in happiness, wherever they may be.

––––––

THE SIGN OF THE STAR
by Dorothy Trimble, P.M. (Ind.)

May be sung to tune of "I'll Take You Home Again, Kathleen"

In many places round the world
There is a flag that's oft unfurled.
Its pure white field no stain should mar.
It bears the sign of Eastern Star.
We took a pattern from the star
That guided Wise Men from afar.
Each point became a shining ray,
A chart and compass for each day.

To our beloved red, white and blue
Was added green and yellow, too.
And every color is the key
To secret signs twixt you and me.
Our open Bible holds the creed
For all mankind — fills every need,
And from its holy pages are
The precepts of our Eastern Star.

On foreign soil, in native land,
In every state, a loyal band
Who, by this sign, proclaim they are
The Order of the Eastern Star.

CEREMONIES

LIGHT

An Installation Addenda
by Bessie Bissett

Speaker (preferably a Past Matron) who carries a large purple or white candle which she lights as she approaches the East to address Star Points. If safety candle is not used, tie a lace paper doily over the end with ribbon to protect her hand from the drippings. As she approaches each Star point, she lights their candle.

Star Points rise when Speaker addresses them and resumes seat when she has finished.

Properties needed: In the East, bowl of five S.P. colors and 5 slim candles. At each S.P. pedestal, a bowl of that color flowers with a candle of same color in the center.

SPEAKER: *(from the East)*

Inspiration comes from LIGHT and as we are inspired tonight by the lighting of our central star,

> May the gleanings of our minds be sweet and pure,
> And the reward of our actions measured and sure.

(Approaches Adah, lights her candle while speaking — and each Star Point in turn)

The light of the blue ray bids the telling of the story of Jepthah's Daughter, whose obedience to her Father's vows leaves us in awe at the significance of Fidelity.

Sister Adah,

> I charge you be loyal, faithful and true,
> And add virtues as you travel life through.

(Adah sits down, Speaker goes to light Ruth's candle — same procedure to be followed throughout)

The light of the yellow ray shines and we are reminded of Ruth and devotion. Her duty was one of labor but it was transformed to one of beautiful service because of love.

Sister Ruth,

Toil long and your courage keep,
Love and gratitude is the harvest you will reap.

(Proceeds to Esther)

The white ray gleams with the powerful light of determination, casting the glow of approval upon pure thoughts and righteous deeds.

Sister Esther,

Do keep this banner clean and white,
Proudly unfurled in our sight.

(Proceeds to Martha)

Green represents the light of faith which was in the heart of Martha and must live in the hearts of all who believe in a glorious hereafter.

Sister Martha,

Teach well this lesson: "To rise" is a promise given,
'Tis by faith we gain our home in heaven.

(Proceeds to Electa)

The light of the red ray denotes fervency of purpose, rightfully directed for the good of others and we know that truth, earnestly spoken, will always prevail.

Sister Electa,

Love is charitable, sweet and kind,
It is the essence of all things fine.

(Proceeds to East and lights each candle appropriate to each word)

Worthy Matron,
FIDELITY — CONSTANCY — PURITY — FAITH and LOVE symbolize the teachings of our Order. Combine them all together so that our Order will prosper, now and forever.

Worthy Patron,
Our stability depends upon good fellowship and fraternal love, and these do prevail in our teachings.
Strong and steadfast, help to make that feeling be
And our Star will shine brightly for all to see.

(Faces West to address all)
As we come to our Chapter room and hear the lessons of our Order, may we look for love and find it; may we have our hopes fulfilled; our faith restored; and find that charity abounds.

Faith, Hope and Charity,
But the greatest of these is Charity.

———

TO HONOR 25 YEAR MEMBERS
by Ruth Adams, P.G.M.

Presenting pins, certificates, or other suitable gifts. Short speaking parts for Conductress and Star Points who ask the 25-Year Members to recall long ago when so-and-so were the Star Point officers. Change the words within ( ) to fit the gifts being given.

WORTHY MATRON:
Tonight is an important night for we present ( ) to those

members who became 25-Year Members during the year _____.

Sister Secretary, will you read the names and dates of all who are still members who were initiated or became affiliated in ____ Chapter during the year of ____.

SECRETARY *(reads the list)*

WORTHY MATRON:

Sister Conductress, will you present our 25-Year Members for introduction.

CONDUCTRESS *(escorts them back of Esther's chair, introduces them, and then continues):*

In memory may we now go back
To when you walked in the light
Of our shining Star so beautiful
And heard our stories of honor and right.

(Star Points all turn and face the 25-Year Members. Use name of Star Point officer of 25 years ago in the proper blank.)

ADAH:

Do you remember long, long ago
When you stood at the point of blue
To hear ___ _____ tell Adah's story
Of right and duty to which she was true?

RUTH:

Do you remember that night long ago
When you paused at the yellow ray
As ___ _____ told of Ruth's devotion
And loving service, day after day?

ESTHER:

> Do you remember that long, long ago
> As you stood at the point of pure white
> To hear ___ _____ tell Esther's story
> Of bravery and decision for the right?

MARTHA:

> Do you remember that night long ago
> When you came to the point of green
> To hear ___ _____, as Martha,
> Tell of faith and hope in things unseen?

ELECTA:

> Do you remember long, long ago
> Standing at Electa's ray of love
> To hear ___ _____ tell that story
> Of fervent truth inspired from above?

CONDUCTRESS:

> Yes, we know that you do remember
> And that is why you are here
> To count your years together
> With the friends that you hold dear.
>
> This (   ) is a symbol of 25 years
> Of loving service to Eastern Star.
> We know you will (wear) it with pride and joy
> As the faithful, true members you are.
>
> *(Presents pins, or other suitable gifts)*

SONG: *Long, Long Ago (or other suitable selection)*

WORTHY MATRON:

Sister Conductress, escort our honored members to seats.

ACKNOWLEDGMENT OF A 25-YEAR PIN
by Vee Hansen, P.M.

As I have been sitting here listening to the remarks being made, I could not help but think "I am getting on." I guess you'd call me an "old-timer." Twenty-five years have passed since I was privileged to be initiated in _____ Chapter. Links in our chain have been broken, but new links have been added.

I am proud to be an Eastern Star and proud to be a member of this Chapter, and I shall be honored to wear this 25-Year pin which you have presented.

I've made wonderful friendships through the years and I am grateful for the opportunity of associating with those whose purposes in life are based on the fatherhood of God, the sisterhood of woman, and charity and loving kindness to one's fellowman.

The Order promises us nothing, but we get much, much more than we give and we can gain much enrichment in our life by following these principles following the Golden Rule.

What a wonderful time is life's autumn
When the leaves of the trees are all gold,
When God fills each day, as He sends it
With memories priceless and old.

My memories are priceless and so is this 25-Year pin. Thank you, again.

OUR HERITAGE

A Program for Birthday Anniversary and to Honor
CHARTER MEMBERS
by Ruth Adams, P.G.M.

*Speaking parts for W.M., W.P., Chaplain, Marshal, Star Points
Properties needed: Birthday cake with candles, or cup cakes,
each with a candle; optional, paper hats*

MATRON: Sisters Conductress and Associate Conductress, will
you please present the Charter Members.

*(While this is being done have music softly played.
Suggest: HAPPY BIRTHDAY or MEMORIES)*

MATRON:

Dear Charter Members, it is indeed a pleasure
To greet you here tonight as ___ years we measure.
All through these years you've been faithful and true,
Always loyal, always constant, and always loving, too.

_____ names are listed on the charter which we own and
We know you've watched with pride as we have grown and
grown.
And you, as our Charter Members, are dear to every heart
For 'twas your push and pull that gave us our wonderful
start.

It is a rare privilege to greet you as we celebrate the ___ anniversary of receiving our Charter. In Psalms 16:6 It states:
"The lines are fallen unto me in pleasant places — yea, I have
a goodly heritage."
These words are quite fitting for the members of ___ Chapter,
which is truly a pleasant place and, thanks to you, we have a
goodly heritage of fine traditions.

Before continuing with our program, our Chaplain will lead us in prayer.

CHAPLAIN *(from her station):*

Our Father, we ask Thy blessing upon this Chapter and all its works. Help us to live so that we may prove worthy of the goodly heritage which has been given unto us. We thank Thee for giving us fine leaders in the past and for Thy Book which has ever led us. Bless those members also who are unable to be with us tonight and give us all strength of purpose to serve Thee to Thy Glory, forever. Amen.

MARSHAL:

Yes, we do indeed enjoy a goodly heritage — the Flag of our Country is part of that - and another is that famous Mason who valiantly fought for it — George Washington. He was a true and upright Mason who was initiated in Fredericksburg Lodge No. 4 in Virginia, and was later a charter member of the lodge at Alexandria. The colors in the flag which he carried are three of the Star Point colors and they form a triangle, a symbol of perfection, within our Star.

ADAH:

Like Adah of the blue ray,
My heritage was found to be
The Holy Bible opened wide
To point to the path of fidelity.

RUTH:

Like Ruth of the yellow ray,
You've industrious and constant been
To labor for the cause of good
And let the light shine in.

ESTHER:

> Like Esther of the white ray,
> Your heritage was found to be
> For kindred, friend, country, and God
> The gleaming light of loyalty.

MARTHA:

> Like Martha of the green ray,
> Your hope and faith have been secure
> Upon an abiding trust in God
> To strive for all that is pure.

ELECTA:

> Like Electa of the red ray,
> The heritage of love you taught
> Like a candle burning in the night
> Your zeal was the flame which we caught.

PATRON:

> Dear Charter Members, we've admired you
> Through the passing years,
> For your love, and for your courage,
> And for your progress without fears.
>
> You have set a pattern
> That has proved to be true and right,
> And we'll be ever faithful
> To carry on your light.

MATRON:

> A birthday celebration complete could never be
> Without a cake with candles for everyone to see.

So, in the past few minutes, we've planned a big surprise—
Just turn around, face the West, and open wide your eyes.

*(While they have been facing East, have a table brought in with
cloth, cake with candles, and a chair for each Charter Member,
and a gift at each place. If this is too elaborate, have a small
cup cake with a candle for each one. Have the candles lighted
and while the Charter Members are being seated, all sing
HAPPY BIRTHDAY*

Optional: paper hats)

RAINBOW FAN: Program for Honored Guest
by Ruth Adams, P.G.M.

*Speakers: W.M., W.P., Chaplain, Star Points, A.M. (who
presents the gift)*
*Properties needed: Fan, or frame, onto which the S.Ps. can
quickly fasten small bunches of their color flowers. Have the
stems quite short and each bunch may be wired and ends of
wire slipped through holes already made in the fan or frame.
Scotch tape can also be used.*

MATRON:

I searched through my poetry books hoping to find just the
right lines which would express my joy in welcoming you tonight to let you know how honored we are to have you with us.
Our Star Points are better than I when it comes to rhymes so
I'll leave that to them and, in my own humble way, say I
sincerely welcome you to _____ Chapter, and we are proud to
call you our friend.

PATRON:

Sister _____, for years we have been hearing about your work for Eastern Star, and we have admired you, too, for your ever-ready smile and happy laughter. You are, indeed, a welcome guest and we feel that you belong to us.

MATRON:

Sister Conductress, will you escort our Sister _____

(Escorted first to the Chaplain who has a fan, or frame, onto which the Star Points will fasten their flowers)

CHAPLAIN:

The open Bible is a symbol we hold in reverence. Tonight we have turned to that Book in planning our ceremony. We have it opened to Genesis, 9th Chapter, 13th verse: "I do set my bow in the cloud, and it shall be for a token of a covenant between me and the earth." And, so, tonight, we are forming a rainbow for you as a token of a covenant between our Chapter and you that we will ever be faithful, constant and true.

(Chap. hands fan to Conductress who then escorts Guest to Adah, Ruth, etc. Each S.P. fastens her flowers to the fan after speaking)

ADAH:

I make you a promise
On the blue of our bow,
That we'll be true to you always
As onward you go.

RUTH:

I, too, have a promise
From the shining yellow band
That we'll be ever constant
And by you firmly stand.

ESTHER:
> I bring you a promise
> From the white band of our bow
> That we'll be ever loyal
> To follow you high and low.

MARTHA:
> My promise comes to you
> From the green band of the bow
> Of faith and hope in all you do
> As leadership you show.

ELECTA:
> The promise that I bring to you
> From the red band of the bow
> Is of our love so deep and true
> That we'll never to you say "no."

(Guest is escorted back to the East)

MATRON:
> Now, with our rainbow around you
> Nothing for you can go wrong
> For our love will be your rainbow
> And we'll all sing a happy song.

SUGGESTED SONG: *Rainbow 'round my Shoulder*

ASSOCIATE MATRON *(with gift, goes to East)*:
> At the end of the Rainbow
> What do you hope to find?
> I've always heard there's a Pot of Gold
> And that we have kept in mind.

We know to find the Pot of Gold,
One really has to dig,
So, we decided to save you that chore
And broke into our china pig.

Sister _____, with love from ___ Chapter, I present this little
gift for you.

———

TO OUR DISTRICT DEPUTY
by William L. Nissenson, P.P.

*Speakers: W.M., Conductress and Star Points Can be recited,
chanted, or sung to tune of "Abdul, the Bul Bul Ameer."*

WORTHY MATRON:
Sister _____,
When I see you west of our altar on this night
I just naturally want to do everything right
And I would like to welcome you with fitting and grand
   eloquent oratory,
But I cannot — and so
I'll leave that to those who are free
To properly greet our Deputee.

*Star Points move inward so they will be close to Deputy and
can speak to her directly.*

CONDUCTRESS:
We're happy to meet you
And greet you — we'll treat you

With music and welcoming song.
We're honored to know you
And now — just to show you
We've carried these flowers along! *(present flowers)*

ADAH:

With joy, we receive you,
We hope — and believe you
Will have a good time with us here!

RUTH:

We'll try to be-friend you,
And now — extend you
A welcome that's true and sincere!

ESTHER:

Like Queen Esther, we claim
You're entitled to fame
For serving your District so well.

MARTHA:

Our feelings MUST show —
So, I'm sure that you KNOW
That it's only the truth that we tell.

ELECTA:

You've always stood by us,
That is why all of us
Are with you, where-ever you lead.
The proof has been ample —
You've showed by EXAMPLE
How to "Love One Another" indeed!

SOLOIST: *(Takes position near Deputy and sings suitable song)*

———

THE SPECIAL VALENTINE I SAVED FOR YOU
To Honor Deputy and Lecturer
by Ethel L. King, P.R.M.

Narrator and short presentations by Conductress & Assoc. Cond.
NARRATOR:

A special Valentine sat on a shelf
  In a little country store.
She felt so sorry for herself
  In spite of lace and satin galore.

She tore at her ribbon and rustled her lace —
  And even dirtied her dainty face.
She'd purposely fall down from the rack
  Just to be picked up and set a-right.

She wanted attention and begged someone to choose her —
  She was truly a gorgeous, fragile creature.
She was so unhappy, oh my, yes,
  She yearned for love and a sweet caress.

(Next 2 verses spoken despondently)

"No one wants me, and I go out of season,
  That's what they say is the reason
I've been here all spring and summer, too,
  And now the fall is half-way through!

"I've become so dirty and shopworn here
  That I'll never be wanted at all next year.
Oh me, oh my, alas and alack
  Guess I'll wilt right on this same old rack!"

I couldn't resist her pleading call
  So I took her down from the wall
And I thought — and thought — and thought — in vain
  And, then, I thought all over again.

What would I do with her if she were mine —
  This dear little, sweet little Valentine?
I could look at her — smile at her — read her long verse,
  I could give her another home — for better or worse.

So, that's what I did with my lovely card
  While I tried to think very, very hard
Of someone special to whom I could send her
  Who wouldn't break — nor tear — nor bend her.

The days slipped by so very fast
  Until even January had almost passed,
When the thought came to me quite suddenly
  Of our Grand Lecturer and District Deputy!

They'll visit us near Valentine's Day —
  And we must do what we can to make it gay.
So out of the envelope came my lady in lace,
  I stood her up and looked at her face.

Time does mellow all things they say
  And my lady was no exception that day!
So into my work-box I delved with haste —
  Took out rigging, scissors and paste.

Looked for some paper, lace and "paddin"
  Found what I needed and some pretty red satin.
I clipped, and I pinned, and I sewed, and I basted
  And thought of our guests while I pasted.

And after I finished my labor of love,
  I pinned my lady to the wall above
And thought to myself — you look so sweet and happy
  I'd love to give you to our District Deputy.

We hope this year all the way through
  Will mean happiness to her, and sweet memories to you.
And, then, I thought of another visitor —
  No one else but our Grand Lecturer!

How kind he is, a wonderful friend.
  So, then and there, I decided I'd send   (†)
Our heartfelt greeting on a tray
  To remind him ever of this special day.

To let him know by this token true
  That we wish him health and happiness, too.
And while I straightened up my table,
  I thought — how friendly he is and how able!

How courteous, and how very kind,
  How good, how true, and how refined
Are both our Lecturer and our Deputy —
  THEY spread sunshine through REAL SINCERITY!

> † *Conductress and Assoc. Conductress should leave their*
> *stations at this time, walking quietly and bringing gifts for*
> *Deputy and Lecturer to the East.*

CONDUCTRESS:

  Sister ____, I'm sure we are all glad that the lonely little Valentine was rescued by our Worthy Matron and not left on the shelf, but was all prettied up just for you —
  And with it, this gift carries all of our love for you, too.
    (Presents red satin and lace valentine with gift to Deputy)

ASSOCIATE CONDUCTRESS:

Brother ____, we're proud to remember you
And this wee gift carries all of our love for you, too.

(Presents Lecturer with gift on a large red heart)

THE CROWN OF FRIENDSHIP
To Honor Visiting Officers
by Ruth Adams, P.G.M.

Speakers: 4-line verses by each officer
Properties needed: Gold paper crowns for all being honored who form a circle around the labyrinth. Crowns for the Star Points who are visitors could have a "jewel" of their color pasted thereon.

WORTHY MATRON: Sisters and Brothers,

Of all the jewels of great renown
Most precious are those in Friendship's crown.
So, tonight we join in a greeting hearty, and
We're so glad you've come to our Friendship Party.

All Worthy Matrons step down to begin forming crown; then W.M. says second verse to other W. Matrons after she has introduced them.

We're happy to bid you a welcome true
And say we are glad to be friends with you.
We think you are all jewels of renown
And entitled to wear our Friendship Crown.

(Places gold paper crown upon head of each Worthy Matron)

Use same procedure of joining in crown formation around the altar, introducing guest officers, saying verse and placing crown on head by each officer in turn.

SECRETARY:

In Friendship's Crown, your link is bright
For we count on you to be usually right.
We're happy that you are links in our crown
For you're important in getting the minutes down.

TREASURER:

In Friendship's Crown, the place you hold
Is of great value, for you're "good as gold."
Our chapters do depend upon us
And keeping true accounts is always a plus.

MARSHAL:

In the Crown of Friendship, you have a place
For you form links with stately grace.
We're glad, indeed, to call you friend
And hope we continue this pleasant trend.

CHAPLAIN:

In Friendship's Crown, you shine very bright
As you walk with faith in the path of light.
Tonight, I'm happy to welcome you here
For as Chaplains, together, we walk without fear.

CONDUCTRESS:

> In our Crown of Friendship, we are together
> As links so strong they will stand any weather.
> To call you friend gives me great delight
> As we meet together this Friendship Night.

ASSOCIATE CONDUCTRESS:

> In Friendship's Crown as links of gold,
> Your worth to me can never be told
> For Friendship is precious and cannot be weighed
> On any scales that have ever been made.

ASSOCIATE MATRON:

> The Crown of Friendship gleams tonight
> For you are here as links shining bright.
> To extend my welcome gives me great pleasure,
> For I think you are each a dear treasure.

ASSOCIATE PATRON:

> In Friendship's Crown as links that bind,
> We keep our vows always in mind.
> As companions in the West this year,
> We know we'll soon go into "high gear."

SENTINEL:

> In Friendship's Crown as links of gold,
> We sometimes stand outside in the cold.

But tonight, we're here together inside
And to call you my friend, I take great pride.

WARDER:

The Crown of Friendship shines ever brighter
As the links are clasped tighter and tighter.
I add my welcome to you Warders this year,
It's a pleasure, indeed, to greet you here.

MUSICIAN:

The Crown of Friendship would not be complete
Without musicians to carry the beat.
So welcome, welcome Sisters of Song,
I hope you brought your best voices along!

ADAH:

Now, Friendship's Crown is a golden band
And I add a jewel that is truly grand;
A jewel that shines as a sapphire blue,
A promise of Friendship that is ever true.

RUTH:

To Friendship's Crown of yellow gold,
I add a jewel of splendor bold,
A topaz gem of gleaming beauty,
A promise of friends' devotion to duty.

ESTHER:

> The crown is an emblem we hold ever dear
> Recalling Esther, the queen, without fear.
> So, I add my jewel of dazzling white, and
> A promise of Friendship that will never take flight.

MARTHA:

> To Friendship's Crown of golden sheen,
> I add a jewel of emerald green,
> A jewel of hope, and faith to share
> And a promise of Friendship is my prayer.

ELECTA:

> As a final touch to our Friendship Crown,
> I add my jewel of great renown —
> A ruby red — a jewel of love
> As promise of Friendship from above.

> *All officers have now joined in forming a complete circle
> around the labyrinth.*

WORTHY MATRON:

> Together, we've joined to form a Crown,
> Everyone happy, with never a frown,
> Hand in hand on the path of duty,
> Wearing Friendship's Crown as a jewel of beauty.

ALL: *Blest Be the Tie That Binds*

> *Return to seats*

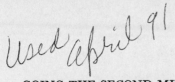

GOING THE SECOND MILE: A Friendly Quiz on FRIENDSHIP NIGHT

by Mrs. J. H. Alexander

Program Chairman asks each officer a question who gives a 2-line answer. Ends with words for a song to be sung to the tune of "What a Friend We Have in Jesus."

CHAIRMAN:

This is Friendship Night, we all can see
But our best friend walked in Galilee.
His heart o'erflowed with love for mankind
And friendliness 'round His pathway twined.

Worthy Matron, do you think that today
Our Chapter could walk in His friendly way?

WORTHY MATRON:

We could, and we can, if we wear a heart warming smile
And without any fuss, go the "Second Mile."

CHAIRMAN:

Worthy Patron, you always walk ahead,
How could we more friendly cheer spread?

WORTHY PATRON:

We could walk on holy ground where He stood;
Like Him, go about doing much good.

CHAIRMAN:

Sister Secretary, you record things won, and lost,

Can you tell us what true friends really cost?

SECRETARY:

The cost is sincere love, and much care,
But it's fully repaid in friendship we share.

CHAIRMAN:

Sister Marshal, you bear our Colors, so grand,
Does that bring real friends to our band?

MARSHAL:

If we hear our flag's words: be tolerant, and just,
We will gain friends to love and to trust.

CHAIRMAN:

Sister Conductress, through our labyrinth's winding,
What are the ties that you hold most binding?

CONDUCTRESS:

The best truth is: Be the friend you would love;
Walk in fellowship sweet to our Home, above.

CHAIRMAN:

Brother Sentinel, you are always at your post —
Can we win the best of life, and its most?

SENTINEL:

Yes, by putting others ahead, whenever we are
And teaching the true kindness of our Star.

CHAIRMAN:

Sister Warder, you guard our portals well.
On building friendship, what can you tell?

WARDER:

We build friendship when we toil and labor,
Taking time to be kind, and sweet to a neighbor.

CHAIRMAN:

Brother Associate Patron, we want advice from you
On keeping our Chapter friendly and true.

ASSOCIATE PATRON:

If we remember and keep the vows we made here,
Our path will glow with star-shine and cheer.

CHAIRMAN:

Sister Associate Matron, you abide in the West —
What friendship road do you think is best?

ASSOCIATE MATRON:

Being a friend is always sharing the load
Of neighboring ones, all along our road.

CHAIRMAN:

Sister Associate Conductress, how would you guide
Into friendship relations, those by our side?

ASSOCIATE CONDUCTRESS:

> The Golden Rule kept in our heart and hand
> Will gain friends for us all over our land.

CHAIRMAN:

> Sister Musician, what is your good word
> For making folks feel friendly and stirred?

MUSICIAN:

> By sharing with others sweet music and serenade,
> We'll have friendly mem'ries that time won't fade.

CHAIRMAN:

> Sister Treasurer, can you suggest a good way
> To keep friendship growing, a little each day?

TREASURER:

> We could stop making gifts to those not in need
> And remember the sad, lonely ones - a good way, indeed.

CHAIRMAN:

> Sister Chaplain, you speak of things ever true.
> What does the word "friendship" mean to you?

CHAPLAIN:

> Living close to Christ and then, hand-in-hand,
> Walking His way - this we can all understand.

CHAIRMAN:

> Sister Adah, you teach us to be true.
> Is this friendship road real easy for you?

ADAH:

> Sometimes our sacrifice must be great.
> As on Adah's mountain, we pray — and wait.

CHAIRMAN:

> Sister Ruth, the harvest of life you know.
> On this friendship path, is it easy to go?

RUTH:

> It brings reward, from the sun and showers,
> And true friends give us happy hours.

CHAIRMAN:

> Sister Esther, in your palace so grand,
> Is comfort found in a friendly hand?

ESTHER:

> Our friends give courage — comfort, too.
> And make our hard tasks easy to do.

CHAIRMAN:

> Sister Martha, you walk by faith, unseen.
> Can you keep friendship alive and green?

MARTHA:

> Faith grows stronger as each one shares
> Tears and joy with a friend who cares.

CHAIRMAN:

> Sister Electa, your cup with love o'erflows.
> Will it keep friends from heartache and woes?

ELECTA:

> Sadness will come to each Sister and Brother,
> But it's eased if we truly love one another.

MUSICIAN *(plays softly): What a Friend We Have in Jesus.*
Members join hands and all sing:

> What a friendly Chapter we have,
> With its fellowship, sincere.
> What a joy to work together
> Spreading comfort, peace and cheer.
>
> Oh, the precious hours we cherish,
> Spent within our Chapter walls,
> Sharing grief, and pleasures, gladly,
> Heeding all our dear Star calls.

———

FISHING FOR FATHER'S DAY
by Dorothy Trimble (Pa.)

Star Points "fish" from an improvised wishing-well with short poles which have wishes fastened to them and each one reads hers as she fishes. Speaking parts for Matron, A.M. and Star Points. Words for a song to be sung to the tune of "Mother."

MATRON:

The second Sunday in May we pay
Our respects to Mothers on Mothers' Day.
We shower her with gifts and flowers,
We sing her praises for hours and hours.
And, then comes June — and are we glad
To pay our respects to dear old Dad!

A. MATRON:

There's no doubt Dad will soon be wishin'
For fishing gear so he can go fishin'.
So, we have invented a wishing-well
That we might his every wish foretell.

ADAH:

Dad's wishin' now for days of ease,
Time to do just what he please;
Wants his gear down from the attic,
A portable radio, with no static.

RUTH:

Wants out where the fishes spawn,
Forget he has to mow the lawn,
Wants a brand new tackle-box —
Not the usual ties and socks!

ESTHER:

Wants one day that folks keep quiet
About someone who needs to diet.

Wants a big steak and french fries,
Ice cream on dutch apple pies!

MARTHA:

Old clothes in which he can relax,
Forget such things as income tax.
Wishes he'd catch there on his hook
Cash to drown that old check book!

ELECTA:

Wishes he could prove someday
All big fish don't get away.
Not at a fishmarket bought —
But THIS is what he REALLY caught!

(Have big pasteboard or artificial fish on end of Electa's Line)

MATRON:

Dad may lay no claim to fame,
But we're proud to wear his name.
Millionaires or digging ditches,
His love and care for us enriches.
That's the reason why we pay
Respects to Dad on Father's Day!

SOLOIST:

F — is for the faith my father taught me,
A — allegiance to my native land;
T — to tell the truth so others trust me;
H — for home and honor both to stand.
E — 's for everything my father gave me,
R — 's for right and right he'll always be.

Put them all together, they spell FATHER,
My Dad, who means the world to me!

———